GENIUS POTENTIAL

Learn How To Identify Your
Genius, Develop Your Genius &
Release Your Genius

_____

By

Dr. Will Moreland

America's #1 Leadership Life Trainer

Table of Contents

Dedication

This book is dedicated to everyone that dares to
live from their _GENIUS POTENTIAL_.

To everyone that dares to live above a label.

To everyone that refuses to allow their past or a
mistake define them.

To everyone that will release their
GENIUS POTENTIAL.

Acknowledgments

I am the result of a lot of love, prayers, forgiveness, mistakes, wins, losses, determination and a host of people that have touched my life over these thirty six years I have been on this planet.

I simply love you all.

Thank you!!!

Kristie Moreland (Wife)
Karah Moreland (Daughter)
Champ Moreland (Son)
Sadie Gray (Mom)
Luvinia Gray (Sister)
Dunjae Wynn (Brother)
To all my other brothers and sisters I didn't get the opportunity to grow up with, love you!!!

There are SO MANY people I want to list right here, but please just allow me to say to everyone that has touched my life, you mean everything to me!!!

To everyone that has helped me spread the
"LIVE GENIUS PHILOSOPHY"
Thank You!!!

Foreword

When I finally got my hands on the final manuscript of this amazing book, I was blown away. I couldn't put it down. Yup... You did it buddy. You have given us a clear, concise manual on one of the most important components of success.

I was born and raised in one of the poorest countries in the world. At the time, Uganda was filled with unimaginable political turmoil, and had an almost non-existent economic base. My environment screamed failure, lack, mediocrity and death. Everyday my circumstances sent me this clear message: "Dennis, you will never amount to anything. You are doomed to a life of penury and privation." So I had a distinct choice before me – to heed the destructive whispers of my decrepit mind or reach deep within to tap into my Genius Potential. I chose the latter, and today, I am living my dream. Its wind has carried me to over 60 nations, speaking hope to millions.

Indeed, I have enjoyed the thrilling ride to the top, but does that mean I am special? Not at all! Is Dr. Will Moreland special? Certainly not! My journey, and the many others in this book, proves that anyone – and I mean ANYONE – can reverse the laws of human conformity and arise from the ashes of shame and decadence to reach the halls of greatness.

Every one of us is pregnant with Genius Potential. Whether black, white, yellow, red or brown, rich or poor, single or married, young or old, all of us! Our job is to recognize it and to unleash it. In this fascinating book, Will lays out a simple process by which anyone can do just that. You will learn how to discover, develop and release your Genius Potential.

I have been privileged to watch Will's life and see him live the principles he shares in this book. I believe it will empower many to achieve greatness for years to come. As you peruse its pages, get ready to be challenged, inspired and equipped to become what you were designed to become – to release your GENIUS POTENTIAL!

Splendid work, Will!

Dr. Dennis D. Sempebwa
President & Founder
Eagle's Wings International
Co-Founder & Director
The Mandate

Preface

Each day Sarah dreaded waking up. Sure she lived in an exclusive neighborhood, had a luxury car, and earned a pretty good income. She loved her family, coming home every night to a wonderful husband and two beautiful children bought a smile to her face. From the outside looking in, one would say that Sarah had the perfect life.

But for Sarah, it was anything but perfect. She had worked hard to climb the corporate ladder. She put in the long hours, did all the right training. Sarah constantly worked to improve herself; but driving that forty-five minutes to work each morning, sapped a lot of her energy. Most days Sarah just went through the motions. Her job was a burden and produced no joy for Sarah.

Harry was a senior vice president for a large semi-conductor company. To think that Harry started off in the mail room and now had the corner office twenty years later was a great accomplishment. Because of his position, Harry traveled a lot, living out of his suit case quite often. Several of his friends would comment how awesome it must be to travel to all those nice places. Harry's usual reply would always be "Comes with the territory." But deep inside, Harry hated all the travel, living from hotel to hotel. He longed to be at home by six o' clock and enjoy a nice home cooked meal. Everyone looked up to Harry; he was a great friend, neighbor and community volunteer. At the office all the junior executives aspired to be where Harry was in his career. But just like Sarah, Harry had a little secret. His life seemed empty and unfulfilled.

Polly was sixty-two years old and recently widowed. Her husband of forty years had recently died of a massive heart attack. Polly had been a stay at home mother for many of the early years of the marriage. Supporting Paul in his career and taking care of the children became her mission in life. Polly and Paul met in college; Paul was studying to be a lawyer, while Polly wanted to be a school teacher. Soon after college, the two married and began their life together. Within the first year of marriage, the couple was expecting their first son, David. By year number five Polly and Paul were welcoming their third child, a beautiful baby girl named Carol. Polly gave all her energy to raising David, Tommy and Carol.

Polly received great joy supporting Paul in his career; and being able to raise their three children was a blessing. But now Polly found herself a little lost. With Paul's recent death, and the children all grown up with their own families, each day seem longer and longer. The children tried to support by calling as much as possible. Carol was the only one living in the same State as Polly now. Carol tried to bring over the children to visit each weekend, which made Polly happy, she loved seeing the grand children, investing time with them made her heart leap. But that joy was short lived because she knew soon Carol would come and she would be in the house all alone again. Polly had an empty feeling on the inside and had no clue how to fill it.

No one was cheering for him. No one was asking for his autograph any longer. Football had been a way of life for Kenny for over twenty years. Since he could remember, he had a football in his hand. He often dreamt of the day that he would play professional football and be a star. Kenny was an outstanding high school football player. In his senior year of high school; every major college wanted Kenny to come play football at their school. As a freshman in college, Kenny earned a starting position on the team. He was closer and closer to his dream of becoming a professional player. Kenny played four years of college football and finished as his schools all time leading rusher.

The night of the NFL draft Kenny was surrounded by family and friends. Everyone was in anticipation as to which team would draft Kenny. Rumors swirled around for weeks that Kenny would be drafted within the first five picks. As the Commissioner came to the podium the excitement in the room was enormous. "And with the first pick, the New York Giants select Ron Hall." Again the Commissioner mounted the podium and said "pick number two, Howard

Rice." Kenny's heart raced as he set on the front row, waiting to hear his name called. The Commissioner steps up, "With the third pick of the 2000 NFL Draft, the San Francisco 49ers select, Kenny Davis." A whale of emotion hit Kenny, it was finally a reality. Kenny was a professional football player.

Fast forward eight years later and Kenny found himself not playing football any longer.

After having a somewhat good career, the pounding his body had taking for over twenty years as a running back, wouldn't allow Kenny to play football any longer. Kenny earned some good money while playing professional football and had managed it pretty well. But without football Kenny was perplexed as to what his next move in life should be. This brought great anxiety to Kenny. With Kenny only being in his early thirties, he wondered what he should do with the rest of his life.

These four stories, all fictitious, are examples of the plight of many people I encounter. Many people feel lost in life, not really knowing why they exist. Countless people wake up each day to give their time and energy to a life they feel doesn't fulfill them. Others find themselves at a cross road because of an unexpected life event. For some it is a career change that has them worried.

For the last decade, I have worked with individuals to help them learn how to *"Live In Victory Everyday."* I am convinced, the only way to experience true and lasting fulfillment is to live from your ***Genius Potential***. I believe that God has placed ***Genius*** in each of us and that ***Genius*** is your key to living a fulfilled life.

As you read and apply the principles of ***Genius Potential***, it will help you identify, develop and release your ***Genius Potential***. This book is not a onetime read; this is what I call a life book. One that you will reference over and over as you learn to release your ***GENIUS POTENTIAL!!!***

Introduction

I kept looking at my passport, then at my plane ticket, back to my passport and then I looked at Kristie, as she was fast asleep. How could she sleep I wondered? Sure the flight was six hours, but we had been on flights longer than this before. The flight home to California from Germany each year was a nine hour flight. So this flight was a piece of cake. I guess I was overly excited because of the destination we were headed. I had traveled to many countries, but this trip for me was the trip of a life time.

As I looked into my passport, I couldn't believe the Visa read Ghana, West Africa. Was I really headed to Ghana, was I really headed to Ghana to speak to hundreds of leaders? Looking out the window of that 747 a tear begin to form in my eye. I wasn't sad; I was overwhelmed at the turn of events that my life had taken in such a short time.

Here I was, a twenty-six year old man going to Ghana, West Africa to speak to pastors, professionals and entrepreneurs about leadership and personal development. How could this be? Just ten years earlier I was on the streets of Hawthorne, California doing all kind of negative activities. Had no direction, no sense of purpose, headed for a long stay in jail most likely. But here

I was getting ready to land some 6000 miles away from Compton, California, my birth place, to the center of civilization, Africa!

I wanted to let out a huge scream, but with all the security measures during flights now, I thought it better to just scream internally. Hours of planning had gone into this trip to Ghana, emails and phone calls went back and forth planning for a four day leadership intensive. The day would be filled with leadership training and in the evenings I would teach principles of faith and hope. I had received all the necessary medical shots, done all the reading I could about Ghana. Talked to some friends who were from the region, I was prepared for an awesome time.

As the plane landed in Accra, Ghana I still could not believe that this little boy raised in Compton, California by a single mother, given a forty percent chance of living at birth, labeled as "Pam's bad son" was in the Motherland. It was unbelievable.

As we departed the plane; I looked over at Kristie and said, "Can you believe this, we are in Africa." How did Bad Will, become Good Will? That's what this book *Genius Potential* is all about, learning to live from the best of you and not the worst of you. How to identify, develop and release your *GENIUS POTENTIAL*. I believe that *GENIUS POTENTIAL* is in all of us, deposited into us by a Genius God. When you read this book, I want you to be inspired to live from your **_GENIUS POTENTIAL,_** what I call the **_"GENIUS LIFE!"_**

This book is about adopting a philosophy I call the **"LIVE GENIUS PHILOSOPHY".** The philosophy is a choice to "_Live In Victory Everyday while Getting ENgaged In Unique Significance._" I made this choice almost 20 years ago and it guides me everyday. Everything doesn't go as I plan all the time, but I choose not to develop a negative attitude, rather I choose to learn, forgive, forget or whatever it takes for me to stay on track to live a significant life.

For me life is not only about being successful, but being significant. Success is more personal, what you have done and achieved, but significance is what you do for others, it means to impact, rather than impress.

-Dr. Will Moreland

CHAPTER ONE

Redefining Genius

"Learning to live from the best of you will be the greatest gift you leave. Live to leave a lasting legacy."

When you hear the word genius what thoughts conjure up in your mind? Who comes to your mind? People like Ludwig Van Beethoven, the great classical composer. Maybe you think of Socrates the brilliant philosopher, Mark Twain the writer, Henry Ford the radical auto maker or Sarah Walker, the first black millionaire. The list could go on and on of individuals I could add to this list of people we consider being geniuses. But have you ever considered yourself a genius? Probably not! Why is that? Most likely it is because you think like I thought for many years, that geniuses were a special group of individuals in the world. People like the great entertainer Michael Jackson, the innovator Steve Jobs of Apple, Inc or Steven Spielberg the well known movie director are usually the people who come to mind when you hear the word genius right. I want you to do me a favor; before we go any further in this book, I want you to add your name right here:

_____ is a **GENIUS!**

I have a very good reason for asking you to write your name in that space. Read the line to yourself, now read it out loud. Does it make you feel uncomfortable? You never considered yourself a genius huh? But from now on your name is listed in a book about geniuses.

The dictionary defines genius in several different ways.

1. An exceptional natural capacity of intellect, especially as shown in creative and original work in science, art, music, etc.
2. A person having an extraordinarily high intelligence rating on a psychological test, as an IQ above 140.
3. Natural ability or capacity; strong inclination: a special genius for leadership.

Look at definition number three, it says genius is natural ability, and we *ALL* have that. For the longest time I focused on the first two definitions and only thought of people like Albert Einstein the renowned physicist, Pablo Picasso one of the greatest artist of all time and Miles Davis the Jazz legend as geniuses. If a person could paint extremely well, play an instrument, or sing exceptionally well, these were the geniuses in my mind.

Why do we admire these people so much? Certainly they all have accomplished some great and amazing things and have received notable recognition for their accomplishments. You would be sadly mistaken to think that these are the only geniuses who have walked the earth. The person reading this book, **YES YOU**, have the opportunity to release your *Genius Potential* and Be Genius!

Genius is...

...living from your natural ability
...serving from your passion
...developing your gifting to be
    used uniquely
...that special something deposited
    into you
...your ability to affect
    environments

And my personal definition of genius that I use is **"Getting ENgaged In Unique Significance.™"**

Have you ever heard of Isha Cogborn, Pam Perry, Eric Thomas, Stephanie C. Harper or Dennis Sempebwa? What about Joyce Dodson, Deborah Hunter, or Alex Ellis? How about Mechelle Tucker, Allyson Byrd or Lisa Nicole Bell? Heard of Marquez Hughley, or John Shumate? Ok last try, how about Vernet Joseph?

If you did a Google search most would show up, but they are not people we would consider famous person. These are individuals I call my *"Everyday Geniuses."* Individuals like you and me that if you passed them on the street there wouldn't be a big entourage following them, people wouldn't be screaming out their names or asking for autographs, well maybe a few of them. But these are individuals that have learned to live from their *Genius Potential.* They have learned to do what I'm going to teach you in this book. They have identified and continue to develop their *"Genius Potential"* and release it to the world in their own unique way.

It was hard for me to believe someone I considered to be an average Joe as myself could become great, do amazing and significant things in this world and even be considered a GENIUS. It wasn't until I read a particular scripture in the Bible and it totally begin the process of transforming my mind and thinking. The beginning steps to all true change.

The more I begin to meditate on the scripture, the more what I read became truth to me. My inner computer, my hard drive was being reconfigured to see myself in a new light.

It's funny how you can read or hear something over and over and then one day it all makes sense. It clicks for you. Well that's what happened for me and the more I begin to agree with the verse the more evidence and proof I received. The evidence was everywhere.

I'm sure you want to know the scripture right? If you are somewhat familiar with the New Testament of the Bible then you may know about the Apostle Paul. He was a great student and teacher. And one day he made this statement;

"For I would that all men were even as I myself. But every man hath his proper gift of God, one after this manner, and another after that."
1 Corinthians 7:7

Paul said that every man hath his proper gift of God. That gift is what I call your *Genius Potential*. The interesting thing about this verse is when I studied it, Paul was referring to him being a single man and having no desire to be married. He recognized that this was a gift, this *Genius Potential* allowed him to be focused on being a missionary and fulfilling his life purpose.

When you are focused, focused on your purpose in life, you can produce at a higher rate. Distractions have less power over you and like a laser your focus helps you cut through obstacles that would stop the unfocused and non-committed individuals in life. When a person has focus that is harnessed toward a real goal they are virtually unstoppable. My definition for **FOCUS** is:

"Fixed **On** Continued **Unique** Service."

When I studied the word gift out, it literally is talking about a unique quality, a genius. And *EVERYONE* has been given a genius. However, you may never benefit from this genius if you are not aware that you have *Genius Potential* and your ability to develop your *Genius Potential* impacts the quality of your life.

> *"When a person's focus is harnessed they are virtually unstoppable"*

What you believe about yourself will greatly influence how you perform in life. Our actions are directly associated with our belief system. There are four major things that shape our beliefs, let's look at them.

The more you understand what shapes your belief system you can protect your belief system.

Belief Shaper #1-Environment

The environment you grow up in plays a major role in shaping your belief system. In most inner cities of America, many young black males believe that the only way to become rich is through entertainment, sports or selling drugs. This directs their activities and what they focus on. When I travel to India, the environment promotes education, so many of the youth focus on their education and getting into great secondary schools.

Belief Shaper #2- Authority Figures

Whom ever you deem to be an authority figure in your life will shape your belief. Parents, teachers, clergy and friends usually assume this role in an individual's life and the information that is passed down becomes a person's belief.

Belief Shaper #3- Repetitious Information

The information you allow yourself to hear over and over again works to shape your belief. The music you listen to on a constant basis will influence you, if you allow negative talk and images into your environment, they will affect your belief system. We will believe what we continuously hear. Faith comes by hearing, so the more you hear something the more it becomes a part of your belief system.

Belief Shaper #4- Personal Experiences

What happens to you in life and how you perceive it will shape your belief system. As an example, if you were bit by a dog when you were a young child, most likely as an adult you will not like dogs. Your belief system tells you that dogs are bad and they bite. At the same time your neighbor has ten dogs and has never been bitten, so they love dogs.

The Talker

Let me give you a more modern example of this *Genius Potential*. The more you give into the idea that we **ALL** have *Genius Potential*, you will be able to identify it wherever you go. If you have a television, you have most likely heard of Oprah Winfrey, the award winning talk show host.

Now be honest with me, have you ever said, "I can't believe they pay Oprah all that money to sit on a couch and talk." We all talk on a daily basis, but none of us earn what Oprah earned to do it. Even people in the same industry didn't earn the type of money Oprah did when she had her talk show.

> *"When You Identify Your "Genius Potential", You Can Maximize Your Time and Efforts."*

So what was the difference? Oprah learned her

Genius Potential was the ability to connect with people. People felt comfortable with Oprah, they felt they could open up to Oprah.

Even though there was a studio audience and millions of people watching, the guest felt as though it was just them and Oprah. Many people viewed Oprah on a weekly basis. As she interviewed her guest, she asked questions her audience wanted to know. This was a skill she developed as a part of her *Genius Potential*.

Oprah learned how to place her *Genius Potential* in the right environment to produce the maximum return. We will talk about placing your *Genius Potential* in the right environment in a later chapter. The more you grab a hold that *Genius Potential* is a person's natural ability to excel, you start seeing *Genius Potential* in yourself and in others as well.

The Enjoy Work Expert

The problem for most of us is that we have the wrong image of who can be a genius or who is a genius. Remember I asked you about Isha Cogborn, one of my *Everyday Geniuses*?

Isha was a teenage mother who many thought was going to end up being another welfare statistic. She defied the odds to become a very successful global communications and branding manager for a $50 billion dollar company after returning to college with her son on her hip, as Isha would say. "My son should have received a degree as well for all the times I took him to class with me," Isha recalls. By all accounts, she looked like she was living the dream. With a respectable home, nice car and all the outward "success trimmings", Isha was still miserable. She suffered from severe work-related stress and developed a chronic illness. After surgery and a four-month medical leave from her job, Isha had time to really examine her life and ask the right questions. Not what could I do to get promoted to earn more money and buy more fancy things, but what is my passion and what was I really created to do.

Isha found the answers and began figuring out what her personal and professional life would look like if she was walking in her purpose. She developed her "exit strategy" – figuring out exactly what she needed to change instead of just dreaming about it. On January 14, 2009, Isha found out she was being downsized. Now

> **Place Your Genius Potential In The Right Place.**

for most people this would have been a devastating blow, but not for Isha. She wanted to invest the rest of her life helping people avoid the trauma she experienced by living a life that didn't bring fulfillment, a life on default instead from her *Genius Potential*. So the very next day, she ordered new business cards and prepared to launch Epiphany Institute – a training and development company that helps others live the professional lives they thought they could only dream about. Isha started living from her *Genius Potential.*

Recently I had lunch with Isha and we got a big laugh because she had just returned from doing some training for the company that laid her off and received a nice pay check for her services. What a gratifying feeling to be living from your *Genius Potential.*

Living from your *Genius Potential* is the only way to live life. It brings so much joy to you. What do the Apostle Paul, Oprah and Isha have in common? They identified, developed and released their *Genius Potential.* They learned the *"Genius Formula"* and acted on it.

"Asking the right questions will produce different answers."

GENIUS INSIGHTS

1. Everyone has a natural ability that they can develop into Genius.

2. When you know your *Genius Potential*, you can maximize your time, energy and efforts.

3. Your ability to develop your *Genius Potential* impacts your life.

4. What you believe about yourself will greatly influence how you perform in life.

5. Asking the right questions will produce the right answers.

6. Settle on the truth that EVERYONE has *Genius Potential* on the inside of them.

7. Gratification comes from releasing your *Genius Potential.*

In your own words, who is a Genius?

_____

_____

_____

_____

Can you list some geniuses you know?

_____

_____

_____

_____

What is your _Genius Potential_?

_____

_____

_____

_____

CHAPTER TWO

You Are a Genius

"The potential of every tree starts in a seed that must be planted to grow."

I don't know how you came to be reading this book, perhaps you are a family member or a friend. Maybe we met on a social media site; maybe someone gave you this book as a gift. Maybe the title captured your attention and you wanted to examine what I had to say. However you came to be reading this book I am thankful and grateful. I truly believe it will enhance your life and usher you into a living that you never thought possible before.

The ideas, concepts and principals I share with you are things I live and have incorporated in my life. They are not new ideas, concepts or principals; they have been around for ages. If you have read the Bible or any of the foundational books on human potential, personal develop and self help, you will see the same principals. Because of those reasons I almost didn't write this book. I constantly told myself that there is enough material on this subject. But I was listening to master motivator Jim Rohn one day, and he said *"It takes many voices to convey the same message, because we all don't respond to the same voice."*

So for that reason, I lend my voice to the many others that have echoed over the years that there is greatness in each one of us. That the potential for better is available to all of us. That time and chance, the opportunity to advance our lives will come to each of us. From the beginning of time when God spoke to Adam and said "Have dominion over the earth," to the great Les Brown saying to an audience of 80,000, "Better is possible"; I Will Moreland say to you, that there is *GENIUS POTENTIAL* on the inside of you.

Get Rid of the Doubt

You may still think that I am stretching it a bit far to say that there is *Genius Potential* on the inside of you. And the reason you are saying that is because your belief system is still telling you that a genius is some "uniquely gifted person" and the rest of us mere mortals must sit around and be amazed at their great talents.

Whenever I present this topic in a seminar or conference it never fails that at the end someone will come up to me and give me a list of reasons why it won't work for them. How it is impossible for them to live from their *Genius Potential*. You may be having the same uncertainties. That's because your hard drive is receiving new information and it may be overloading your current belief system. I have identified several causes why people find it hard to accept the *"Genius Potential Theory."*

1. Past failures
2. Other peoples failures
3. Bad habits you have developed
4. Comparing yourself to others
5. Limiting perception of yourself
6. Negative words spoken to you
7. Passing of time, you think it is too late

I too at some point looked at all of these causes and made excuses for me not to live from my *Genius Potential*. I will share with you how I overcame these doubts and fears. Remember

"Have more confidence in God's wisdom than in your past failures, mistakes and disappointments."

that verse I shared earlier, 1 Corinthians 7:7. I began to renew my mind by reading that verse. I read it over and over. I even wrote it down in a note book over a thousand times until it was implanted in my subconscious mind. Then I came across another verse to add to it. It was amazing the evidence I kept finding to support this new philosophy. I was born to be a **GENIUS**!

"Every good gift and perfect gift is from above, and cometh down from the Father of lights, with whom is no variableness, neither shadow of turning." (James 1:17)

I begin to transform my belief system to believe that God had placed my *Genius Potential* on the inside of me. I started to have more confidence in God's wisdom than in my past failures, mistakes and disappointments. Hopefully as I share not only my story, but others that have chosen to live from their *GENIUS POTENTIAL*, you will be motivated and inspired to make the necessary adjustments in your life and join the minority group that has made the decision to live as a **GENIUS**.

The renewing process was just the beginning steps, but it was a vital step. The more I believed that I had something special to offer the world, the more support I found to back it up. You have to understand whatever you believe you will find evidence to back it up, even if it is an untruth. For years people believed that the world was flat. That it was impossible to walk on the moon. That the human body would explode if it ran a mile in four minutes or less. All these have been proven to be wrong.

Learning and applying the *"Genius Potential Formula"* will allow you to live from your *Genius Potential*. As you continue to read this book, see if you can identity what the formula is. I will reveal the formula in a later chapter, but see if certain concepts leap out at you. In each chapter and in each story, you will see parts of the formula at play.

It Doesn't Matter Where You Start

I was raised in Compton, California to a twenty-one year old single mother of one. My father was fifty years old and was known as a ladies' man. I am his tenth child I believe and I have some siblings that were born after me. To top it off, when I lived in Compton, it was reported as the most dangerous city in the United States.

> **"Whatever you believe you will find evidence to back it up."**

On the surface it doesn't look like the ingredients for a promising future I know, but over the years this is what I have learned. No one gets to choose their parents, the neighborhood they grow up in or the family they are born into. You don't get to choose whether you are born in

America or China, the "Right Side of the Tracks or the Wrong Side of the Tracks." It is what it is.

But there comes a day when you do get to choose what path in life you will follow. Up until several years ago I would often say I had a rough upbringing; that I lived in the ghetto and life was terrible. I have since altered my statement to say I didn't have the most ideal upbringing. Because I have traveled to some places and talked with many people about their childhood and I can truly say, although we didn't have much, we always had enough.

Now growing up in Compton was no bowl of Fruit Loops, don't get me wrong. With the constant gun shots, drug dealing and gang wars, you had to grow up pretty fast. Like almost every other kid I just learned how to maneuver in this environment. You learned where you could go, what streets to walk down and which ones to avoid. In short it became a way of life; I learned survival techniques long before I joined the Army. They called Compton a war zone.

One of the interesting things about growing up in Compton was when I would tell other people I lived in Compton; the reaction was always funny to me. I knew I lived in a not so glorious place, but it didn't seem as bad as everyone made it seem. It was home. I was comfortable.

I have some good friends from Liberia, and one evening at a dinner, we were discussing our childhoods and I was amazed to hear the horror stories they told about growing up in Liberia during the Civil War that occurred in their country. In Compton we had drive-by shootings and occasionally a neighborhood fight, but the stories my friend told far outweighed anything I had experienced.

> ### *"One Day You Have To Decide To Live Different."*

I recall one story they told me about rebel forces invading the village where they lived. In the dark of night, they could hear the rebels burning down the houses. My friend recounted her mother waking her and her siblings up and running through the night air. Not really knowing where they were headed, just knowing they had to escape.

I asked my friend how they lived in such torment and fear. She replied, "It became a way of life." Interesting how such horrible conditions and circumstances can become a way of life for so many. Each week I speak to countless people that absolutely resent their job, their communities and their lives for the most part. But they have done what my friend and I did; they have learned to live in the mist of chaos. Feeling as though they are trapped, doomed to live a life of mediocrity.

Unwilling to believe that better is possible. Not allowing their environment to motivate them, instead of arrest them. Choosing not to be the captain of their life. Complaining about the troubles, instead of searching for answers and looking for solutions. If this sounds like you, hopefully this book will provide a way out. Give you a blueprint for a better and much more fulfilling life.

I didn't write this book to make you feel better about your bad situation, but the ideas, concepts and principals in this book will allow you to develop a winning philosophy in life. When you come to realize that learning to live from your *Genius Potential* is the key to joy and fulfillment and that the Universe is designed to support your *Genius Potential*, life takes on a whole new meaning. I believe that God knows that the *Genius Potential* on the inside of you is so powerful, that it doesn't matter where you are born, your *Genius Potential* can make opportunities for you and usher you into new arenas.

I love this poem by C.S. Longenecker,

If you think you are beaten, you are,
If you think you dare not, you don't.

If you like to win, but you think you can't,
It is almost certain you won't.
If you think you'll lose, you're lost,
For out in the world we find,
Success begins with a fellow's will.
It's all in the state of mind.
If you think you are outclassed, you are,
You've got to think high to rise,
You've got to be sure of yourself before
You can ever win a prize.
Life's battles don't always go
To the stronger or faster man.
But soon or late the man who wins,
Is the man who thinks he can.

Because in life it really is the person that thinks they can, that really gets things done in life. Understand that where you start really doesn't matter. There are people that started off at the top and finished at the bottom and vice versa. That Jewish Rabbi by the name of Jesus, started off in a manger, but finished as Savior of the World.

An Uncommon Genius Rises

Mother Teresa who became an inspiration to millions around the world started off in a small city in Macedonia. At the age of twelve she had a strong sense of calling on her life that she should be a missionary. When she left her home at the age of eighteen, she began what I call her journey to releasing her *Genius Potential.*

After teaching for several years and seeing the poverty of the people in Calcutta, India, she requested permission to leave her position as a teacher and start to work with the poorest in the city. She had no formal training to work on the streets, no finances or blueprint, just a sense of purpose. Mother Teresa just started doing what she felt was right for her. Ill-regardless of the lack of financial backing, ill-regardless of her lack of experience, the desire to pursue her passion was enough.

Some years later Mother Teresa's actions were rewarded when she was granted her own order by the Holy See. The Missionaries of Charity, which in turn became an International Religious Family by a decree of Pope Paul VI in fifteen short years.

From her humble beginnings in Macedonia, Mother Teresa was the seed that has blossomed into a worldwide recognized organization serving millions around the world. She has received some of the highest awards a human being can receive, Pope John XXIII Peace Prize and the Nehru Prize for her promotion of international peace and understanding. She also received the Balzan Prize, the Templeton and Magsaysay awards, and the Nobel Peace Prize. Finally being beatified by Pope John Paul II.

Is Mother Teresa much different than you and I? Was there a special call just on her life? In no way do I think that each of us will win the Nobel Peace Prize, but we all can win the *"Release Your Genius Potential Prize."*

That's what this book is all about, teaching you how to act on that *Genius Potential* on the inside of each one of us. Mother Teresa did what each of can do, and that is serve from our *Genius Potential*.

A Soldier's Journey

Vernet learned how to serve from a Haitian father that instilled into his children that it is your duty to serve your fellow brother. Coming from a long line of men that have served in the military, it was a natural decision for Vernet to join the United States Army.

I met Vernet almost twelve years ago while we were serving together in Germany. From day one I felt his energy. His drive to be his best was evident to everyone that he came in contact with. His can do attitude is contagious.

Dr. Joseph "**Mr. Productivity**" as he is known around the world today has been my close friend for all these years. He would probably say I have taught him many things over the years, but the deposits have been mutual. He is a reservoir of ideas and inspiration. Watching him turn his natural ability to serve others into a major speaking platform has been amazing.

When Vernet came to me and inquired about starting his speaking career two years ago, I was excited, but naturally thought he was talking about when he retired from the military in a few years. He quickly corrected me and said "No, I'm ready now." I was thinking to myself, he must have forgotten that he was still on active duty. Then I wondered if he decided to leave the military to pursue his passion of developing others in a different arena, since he was already developing leaders in the military.

But in his "**Mr. Productivity**" way, he looked at me and said "I got this, too easy." Remember when I told you that the Universe will respond to your *Genius Potential*? When we started to lay the foundation for his speaking platform a funny thing happen. The military decided to allow Vernet to attend college at home. This meant that he was able to leave the military base, return to his family in Arizona and for two years live as a civilian. This provided the essential time he needed to build his speaking platform, to release his *Genius Potential.*

If you are really serious about doing something, the time, resources and way will all be made available to you. Anyone can find excuses why something can't happen, but geniuses find a way to make it happen. So what did the super producer "**Mr. Productivity**" do with this new opportunity? He not only built a major speaking platform, traveling across the United States to teach on the subject of productivity. He wrote and published two books. Started a business and became the Chief Operating Officer of another company. Oh, did I forget to mention while being a husband and father to two young girls.

And to top it all off, he maintained a grade point average of 3.5 while obtaining his degree in business. That's why we call him **"America's #1 P3 Expert"** and **"Mr. Productivity."** Just another example of an *"Everyday Genius."*

> **"There comes a day when you do get to choose what path in life you will follow."**

GENIUS INSIGHTS

1. The principles to release your *Genius Potential* have been around for years.

2. *Genius Potential* is in EACH of us.

3. Have more confidence in God's plan for you then your past mistakes.

4. You don't get to choose where you start, but you can decide where you finish.

5. Learn to search for answers instead of excuses.

6. The Universe is designed to support your *Genius Potential.*

7. We can ALL win the "Release Your *Genius Potential* Prize."

When you give it some thought, can you see
Genius Potential **around you?**

_____

_____

_____

_____

What Do You invest most of your time doing?

_____

_____

_____

_____

Are you on the path to living a Genius Life?

_____

_____

_____

_____

CHAPTER THREE

Identifying Your Genius Potential

"The more I believe and act on that belief, the more I receive."

By now I hope you are wondering about how you can live from your *Genius Potential*. Are you asking yourself what is my *Genius Potential*? These are questions that will help propel you to release your *Genius Potential*. In this chapter I want to help you identify your *Genius Potential*. Remember what Paul said…

"For I would that all men were even as I myself. But every man hath his proper gift of God, one after this manner, and another after that."
1 Corinthians 7:7

So the question is not do I have *Genius Potential* in me, the question becomes what is my

Genius Potential? When I talk to people about identifying their *Genius Potential*, they have a difficult time because they are still stuck at the thought or image of an Einstein or Picasso. Remember, genius is operating from a natural passion. Come on say it with me,

"Genius is operating from a natural passion"

Think back for a moment to your child hood. What did you enjoy doing? Take a few moments and really think about it. There have always been small clues to your *Genius Potential*. I know for me, people would always say "he loves to talk." Not knowing that talking would be a huge part of my future. Did you like helping a parent in the kitchen? Maybe working on the car in the garage, take a moment and think about it. Close your eyes and think back to what people have always associated you with in a positive way.

Did you get a vivid picture? When you really think back, you will see your *Genius Potential* has always been there. For most of us we have grown up in a system that teaches us to be copy cats. From early on in our schooling we are compared to other students, evaluated against other students and given test that may not identify our *Genius Potential*. From the time you started school you have been asked to fit into a box, a certain standard. And you have been graded according to that standard most of your life. The current education system is designed to grade as if we are all the same, although it is clearly known that there are several learning styles.

Many adults find themselves trapped by a label they received as a child. I know you remember as a child being asked the question "How are your grades?" Remember that tight feeling some of you got when you had to say not so good, I got a "C" in math or science.

This formed a subconscious pattern in your mind to make you think that you were inadequate compared to everyone else. I remember sitting in the auditorium loathing the idea of watching other students receive their academic awards for excellence, "Being a Genius" in school. It wasn't until we went on the playground where I was faster than everyone did I feel like I was important.

When you are looking to identify your *Genius Potential*, don't look for what the masses reward, look for what makes you come alive. I was a horrible test taker, but I had the ability to grasp concepts well and explain them, but when it came time to taking test, I would freeze up. What I learned later in life was that I did better on test that covered subjects I was passionate about.

"Find Out What Makes You Come Alive."

Everyone Has It

Have you ever watched an advertisement for an upcoming movie? What do they highlight? Usually it is the movie star with the big name. If not the movie star, they will highlight the director or producer with the big name. You never see the camera person or set directors name. But these individuals are just as important and need to perform as well as the movie star and director for the movie to be a success.

When I buy a DVD one of the first things I like to watch is the special features. I love learning about the process it took to make the movie, the many moving parts it took to bring the movie to the big screen. This is when you get to see *Genius Potential* at work; you get to see **"Everyday Geniuses",** people you would never notice on the streets. One movie that comes to mind is Big Mama's House that starred Martin Lawerence. But Martin wasn't the person that caught my eye when I watched the behind the scenes footage of the movie.

When I was watching the special features the individuals that grabbed my attention were the team of make-up artists and special effects people that worked on the movie. The excitement they expressed in being able to work on this project was fascinating to me. Greg Cannom the special effects make-up artists on the movie saw it as a challenge to turn Martin into a 350 pound woman to play the part of Big Mama. A true genius trait, to see obstacles as challenges to conquer.

The director talked about Martin being a comedic genius, so they knew they had to match him up with a make-up artist of the same caliber. Many of you have heard of Martin Lawrence, but how many of you have heard of Greg? Right! But in the film world, Greg is a genius at what he does, Greg as been nominated nine times for an Oscar, the highest award in the movie industry, winning three times. *Genius Potential* is not about being in the lights or headlines, it's about doing what brings you joy.

Another *"Everyday Genius"* I learned about was Linda Benavente-Notaro; she created the fat suit that Martin wore in the movie that transformed him into Big Mama. Linda is the same person that transformed Robin Williams into Mrs. Doubtfire, a movie from the early 90's. Linda is also known for her **Genius Work** on movies like the Hook, X-Men, Tron, Fantastic 4 and White Chicks.

"Genius Potential Is Not About Being Center Stage."

Think for a moment, what if the studio paid to have the best actor, best director and best set director, but hired inadequate camera personnel or supporting actors. You wouldn't have a very good movie. *Genius Potential* is something we want to experience everywhere we go, from everyone we encounter.

How Do We Identify Our Genius Potential?

Before I give you some key points to identifying your *Genius Potential*, let me tell you about John Shumate. If you are a basketball fan the name may be familiar to you. For you others, you may not be a basketball fan, but you may have heard of the legendary coach John Wooden of UCLA fame. Coach Wooden's UCLA Basketball Teams won an unmatched seven strait NCAA Basketball Championships and 10 in a 12 year span. Known as the **"Wizard of Westwood"** John Wooden is a genius in his own right.

During his coaching years Coach Wooden led UCLA on an 88 game winning streak; yes you read that right, 88 in a row. So the obvious question is always what team finally beat UCLA to end their streak? Insert the Notre Dame Basketball Team and John Shumate the team's starting center. I call John the gentle giant. Standing 6'9 inches tall, he is one of the most humble men I have ever met. But put him on the court and you meet a new person, a man that has battled on the basketball courts with some of the great centers of all time.

John's genius is the ability to inspire and touch people in a special way. Listen to him talk and immediately you know what I'm talking about. Hearing him talk about his upbringing by a strict religious father, from having to sneak to play basketball as a teen and you will be inspired to be your best and release your *Genius Potential*! As a husband, father, player, coach, mentor and friend, John touches people in a unique way. I love hearing John share the million of stories he has from a career in basketball that spans over 30 years, John is simply **GENIUS**!

Every time John takes the stage to speak at events, people are in awe, as he captures the attention of the audience; his sincere presence will draw you in and have you at the edge of your seat. Having John as a friend is a true treat, but the greater joy is watching him release his *Genius Potential* to the world.

Have you been thinking about what your *Genius Potential* is? It's what makes you feel alive, it's natural to you. It's what you naturally gravitate toward doing. What do you do and people cheer for you?

"There Is An Opportunity To Release Your Genius Potential, Look For It."

Personally, my *Genius Potential* is teaching. More specifically teaching on leadership, business and personal development. I naturally look for opportunities to teach. Writing books is a platform I use to teach. My radio show, **"The Dr. Will Speaks"** Radio Show was another platform I used. My Facebook, Instagram, Pinertest and Twitter pages are platforms I use to teach.

Take another moment and think, what is your *Genius Potential*? Write it down.

I really come alive when I:

_____

_____

_____

_____

There are some tests, assessments you can take to help give you some clarity in identifying your *Genius Potential*. I have taken them over the years and they assisted me in pin-pointed for myself what area I should focus on.

The first test is called your Spiritual Gifting Assessment. Even if you do not consider yourself a spiritual person, it can shed some light about you. I have taking the assessment several times over the years and my results have always been the same. My three top results have been Leadership, Teaching, and Exhortation.

The second assessment test I used is the Myer-Briggs Assessment. Another good tool to help identify your natural bent. Learning about yourself is an essential key to living from your *Genius Potential*. When you really learn about you, you are no longer motivated by outside opinions of others. Your decision making is absent from public opinion. Take these two assessment test and see if they are in line with what you were feeling all along.

Remember, *Genius Potential* is living from what comes natural to you.

She Had No Other Choice

You are comfortable on your job, nothing to write home about, but it is paying the bills and giving you a little extra money. Then one day you find yourself laid off, living with a friend and you have little children staring you in the face. After several months you need to leave where you are living and you only have $99 dollars to your name. What do you do? You write a book and you start your own magazine right? Well that's what you do if you are Stephanie C. Harper, publisher of CAREER Magazine. Faced with some of the greatest challenges in her life, Stephanie took a step back and said to herself, "I have played it safe all these years and look where it has landed me." Stephanie decided to live from her *Genius Potential.*

After working in the Human Resource field for over fifteen years, Stephanie knew the ins and outs of that business. Her passion to help other individuals stay on top of their game and career developed. She wanted to equip people with the best work practices and career tips she could find.

Only thing she had to figure out now was how she would reach a mass audience in a short period of time and on a frequent basis. **"Genius Bulb Moment!"** Stephanie decided to launch a magazine. Problem! She didn't have a clue as to what the steps were to starting a magazine. Remember when you are serious, the Universe will respond in your favor. Stephanie went to work, educating herself about the business, investing long sleepless nights. Reading over "How To" manuals and watching instructional videos. Every obstacle was a road block that had to be conquered, because it stood between her and her opportunity to live from her *Genius Potential.*

Stephanie knew what the magazine would mean to so many individuals seeking a wealth of knowledge to stay current with the always changing trends in the 21st Century market place. The work was laborious, but the end result would usher her into her **"Genius Place."** Several years removed from that one bed room apartment she found with her last $99 dollars on a "Move-In Special" Stephanie is living from her *"Genius Potential."*

Let me share with you some keys questions that will help you discover you're *Genius Potential*:

Questions To Identifying Your
Genius Potential:

1. What makes you come alive when you do it?

2. What comes natural to you, you could do it in your sleep?

3. What do you do that brings others great joy and they applaud you?

4. What subjects to you find easy to understand and others struggle?

5. What's the one thing you could do every day and never get tired of doing it?

6. What do others repeatedly tell you, you should be doing?

7. What recurring dream or vision do you continue to have?

8. What really annoys you? Maybe seeing things out of place.

9. What are activities that you have a natural pull toward?

10. What did you visualize yourself becoming as a little child?

Review these ten questions over and over. Continue to seek the answer. The proverb says "Seek and you shall find." Turning your attention to discovering your *Genius Potential* will be one of the most single important things you do in your life. The best you is trapped within your decision to operate from your strength. Your strength is wrapped in your *Genius Potential*.

When you indentify your *Genius Potential* you are in a better position to become more innovative and creative. You create space for yourself in the world. Options are open to you in a grander scale.

GENIUS INSIGHTS

1. The question is what is my *Genius Potential*?

2. Genius is operating from a natural passion.

3. Don't look for what the masses reward, look for what makes you come alive.

4. *Genius Potential* is not about being on center stage or in the headlines.

5. *Genius Potential* is something we want to encounter everywhere we go.

6. Opportunity to release your *Genius Potential* is ALL AROUND.

7. Learning about you is essential to living from your *Genius Potential*.

What Do You Think Your *Genius Potential* Is?

_____

_____

_____

_____

Who Inspires You?

_____

_____

_____

_____

What Are The Last Books You Read; Do They Support Your *Genius Potential*?

_____

_____

_____

_____

CHAPTER FOUR

Living from Your Genius Potential

"Give yourself a reason to wake up each morning."

Every morning I wake up there is a smile on my face because I know today that I am living from my *Genius Potential.* In this chapter I want you to meet some more individuals that have made the shift into living from their *Genius Potential.* Come back to this chapter over and over to be motivated and inspired by these geniuses.

I truly believe all my obstacles, trials, test, experiences and life's journey have prepared me and continue to equip me to live from my *Genius Potential.* As far back as I can remember I have always been identified as a leader with significant influence. Even though I believe we all are leaders, leading is a part of my *Genius Potential.*

Being able to teach what I do and share concepts and ideas about leadership is my passion. Personal and business development is another passion for me. Growing up in Compton and in the inner city helped develop the experiences I needed to become effective in sharing these principals.

Being the only malc in the house, I would commonly hear the term "Little Man." This began to ingrain in me that I had to be the man of the house. I had no financial responsibilities, no real burden to bear, but constantly hearing "Little Man" made me think I really was a man. In the back of my mind I really couldn't do what the other kids were doing, because I was a man. I developed a maturity quite early on in life. I suppose it made me miss some aspect of my childhood, but it helped mold a sense of leadership in me.

Recently I was looking through some files and came across an old report card from high school. I rarely paid attention to my reports cards, but on this day, I read the whole report. One of my teachers made this comment, "Will has Leadership Qualities." Had I been paying attention, I would have inquired more from him about what he saw in me. What if I were placed in some leadership development programs as a youth? How much further would I be today? Parents, pay attention to what your child is doing and what others are saying about them. My daughter shows a love for cooking. She has been banging pots since she was three years old. We encourage her to pursue this passion. Now at the age of nine she can make breakfast, lunch and dinner for herself. I ask her often which culinary school she would like to attend. We encourage Karah to learn all she can. Friends we know that are in the field share recipes with Karah often.

My development could have started a whole lot sooner and I would have been more focused earlier on in my life if my *Genius Potential* was identified. Take another moment and think back, can you remember some things people always observed about you or commented about you? Please don't make the mistake of over-looking the obvious. Remember what comes easy (natural) to you is your *Genius Potential*. When I talk to people about their *Genius Potential*, they get it mixed up with "Making a Living" or a "Career Choice."

The Publisher

I met a young lady named Deborah Hunter one day at church. After a few moments of small talk, I asked her the all important question that no one escapes from if they are around me for more than ten minutes. I said "Deborah, what is your passion." She replied, "Well I have wanted to write a book for about three years now." I looked Deborah in the face and said have the book to me in 30 days. I can't remember how quickly Deborah got the book to me, but it was before the

30 days. Why was she able to get the book finished so fast? Her *Genius Potential* was waiting to be challenged, so it could be released. I hope this book provides the same kind of push for you. Deborah has since gone on to author three more books. But the momentous thing that came from this encounter was that Deborah started her own publishing company. Wrapped up in her writing her book was her *Genius Potential*. Now she helps other authors fulfill their dreams of writing books. Hunter Heart Publishing is becoming a force in the publishing industry.

Deborah thought writing books was going to be her entrance into the **"Genius Zone."** Actually writing her book was just the seed. I laugh every time I go to the web site and see all the authors that are being published by Hunter Heart. Deborah and I talk often and she is continuously developing her *Genius Potential* in order to release it in a magnificent way. Being a book publisher fits her so well. She's always had an eye for editing and grimaces when she sees grammatical errors. Everything that annoyed her was there for her to service. *Genius Potential* leaves clues throughout your entire life look for them.

I wouldn't be surprised to see Hunter Heart Publishing become a *"Genius Business"* in the near future. The blue print is there, the company has a *"Genius Leader"*, there is major opportunity in the publishing industry right now and those that are operating from their *Genius Potential* will rise to the top.

It Went Viral

He was just doing his thing. Challenging and inspiring students in Detroit.

Another *"Everyday Genius"* is my friend Eric Thomas, who has come to be known as the **"Hip Hop Preacher"** around the world and has learned to live from his *Genius Potential* as well. Eric was a high school drop-out, homeless and living a life with no direction. One day he was approached by a man that would later become his mentor and challenged Eric to stop living a pitiful life. He challenged Eric to get back in school, get his diploma and continue his education. Eric took his mentor up on the challenge and went back to school. After Eric received his diploma, he then enrolled in college, an endeavor that would take him 12 years to complete.

A funny thing happened along the way to Eric receiving his degree. Eric found his *Genius Potential!* While Eric was pursuing his degree, he noticed that people would naturally come to him for advice. Young men and women would naturally gravitate to him. As they would explain the struggles they were having as college students, Eric would share his story. Word begin to spread about a guy who had dropped out of high school, but know was pursuing his college degree.

Eric decided to start a group that would meet to encourage the students to keep pressing on. Sensing that he was on to something, Eric created a program for incoming freshmen to help them adjust to college life. During one of these presentations someone recorded Eric speaking to the students about what it took to become successful. Several years later, this video was posted on YouTube. The last time I checked, it was viewed over one million times. Eric's speaking career took off. Eric found out that his *Genius Potential* was inspiring individuals to overcome obstacles to live a better life.

Your *Genius Potential* can be found through struggle, pain, joy, experiences or passion. There is no telling how the *"Genius Bulb"* will go off in an individual's life. Through what Eric experienced, being homeless, dropping out of high school and not having a relationship with his father earlier on in his life, set the blue print for Eric to help millions of people.

"You Can Discover Your Genius Potential In The Struggle."

One more time:

Take another moment and think, what is your *Genius Potential?* Write it down.

I really come alive when I:

_____

_____

_____

_____

Master Your Craft

Talk with Pam Perry for one second and you will see that she is serious about her passion, her *Genius Potential.* Pam is a Public Relations Genius. When she started Ministry Marketing Solutions in 2000, she set a fire to the industry. Working with the best artist and authors in the Christian Community, Pam built her brand and media empire.

Her passion to help others position their products in the market place using social media strategies has now become the stuff that geniuses are made of. Pam receives awards every year for her **Genius Work**. I met Pam on Facebook, and the insight I have gleaned from her has been invaluable. I can count on Pam to send me some great information each week. Challenging me to keep my genius sharp. Here is a personal quote from Pam.

"It's prime time to stir up your gift. Shake off the disappointments of the past. Restore your hope! It is not too late for you – no matter how old you are or what "mess" you have been through."

I love it. The type of fire that needs to be lit under most people for them to start their *"Genius Journey."* I look forward to hearing from Pam and following her all around the web. Listen in on one of her calls or mastermind groups and you will hear the passion. Pam is truly releasing her best to the world by releasing her *Genius Potential*.

Use What You Have

If you are like me, thoughts and ideas come to you all throughout the day. Sometimes a thought or idea will come; and I know I am onto something; it is n idea that I need to develop further. Over the years I have learned not to trust my memory, ideas are worth gold. So I love my mobile device that allows me to write on the spot or record my ideas as they come to me.

"Ideas Are Worth Gold."

While sitting in a restaurant an idea came to Marquez. It was a bit far fetch and very much out of his realm of experience. The idea that came to Marquez was to start a clothing lifestyle company. This wouldn't be any clothing line; it would be one that told a story, set a standard for future customers. Only a few issues to address, and Marquez would be good to go.

First issue, he **KNEW NOTHING** about the clothing industry. See Marquez is a country boy from Opelika, Alabama. Opelika is not a place known for its fashion swag. But the idea was so strong that evening Marquez started to sketch out designs for six ties on a piece of a napkin. Use what you have right! The second issue, Marquez was a full time student at Morehouse College in Georgia, plus working a full time job. No way did he have time to pursue a task as humongous as entering the clothing industry. And to add excitement to this idea, Marquez had no capital.

On the way home the idea wouldn't shake him. That night he turned on this computer, went to the only program that he knew to use to design graphics, Microsoft PowerPoint. That evening he laid the foundation of what would be his first ties to hit the market, once he figured out how to make it all happen.

Between classes and work, Marquez began to educate himself on the clothing industry. The road to learning about the manufacturing process, wholesale versus retail pricing, advertising and so on had begun. I remember a mutual friend made a comment after going to visit Marquez, "I don't

know how he does it; the guy doesn't sleep."
Marquez would track to Morehouse for two
morning classes, dart off to work for six to eight
hours and cap it off with a night class or two. Then
he would burn the midnight oil learning all he
could about the fashion industry.

The new formed company he called
Gigaré. In two short years, the company has taking
off, expanding to other men's ware as well as
women's ware. This year the company launched
an online magazine, **Gigaré Lifestyle Magazine**.
Marquez found his *Genius Potential* that evening.
To teach the world that they are worth more than
meets the eye, to empower individuals to live a
"Crown Life."

Marquez now travels around the nation to
inspire entrepreneurs to pursue their dreams. Just
do your homework and never give up on your
dreams is his message.

This is what we call the process or putting
in the work. From that night in the restaurant to
his first tie around his neck, took four months.
Marquez had designed the ties, found a company
to manufacture them half way around the world
and had his product in his hand. I can't wait to see
where he takes this company, the possibilities are
endless. And it all started with a design on a
napkin.

"Use What You Have."

GENIUS INSIGHTS

1. All your test, trials, joy and pain have equipped you to release your *Genius Potential*.

2. Look for the clues your *Genius Potential* leaves.

3. It just takes a spark to begin your Genius Journey.

4. Start with what you can do; never focus on what you don't have.

5. Give your energy to making your dream come true.

6. Act on your ideas, they are valuable.

What Makes You Come Alive?

_____

_____

_____

_____

Ten Years From Now, How Will You Impact The World?

_____

_____

_____

_____

What Is Your Life Mission Statement?

_____

_____

_____

_____

CHAPTER FIVE

Why Develop
Your Genius Potential

"Practice makes better, not perfect."

Hopefully by now you have identified what really makes you come alive, what is natural to you? If not, go back to Chapter Three and reread the chapter. Did you take the two assessment test I recommended? The remaining chapters will assist you in developing your *Genius Potential*. Remember don't look for what is popular or what society says you should be doing. Look within; close your eyes for a moment, think about what would bring you joy on a constant basis?

Your *Genius Potential* is your answer to a brighter future. Each one of us is born with *Genius Potential* to offer the world. Actually, when you don't identify, develop and release your

Genius Potential, you rob the world of a uniqueness we were supposed to enjoy. Think with me for a moment. Who are some of your favorite singers? I have a few. I love to listen to Sade, Anita Baker, Joyce Dodson and Rachelle Farrell; they are in my top favorites of all time. Two of the names on my list you may recognize right off the top, Sade and Anita. If you are really a student of good music you will probably know Rachelle. But you may have never heard of Joyce Dodson, I met her while I was living in Germany. Joyce was the lead singer in our church. Joyce has a voice that is uniquely genius.

I love Joyce's voice, but I wouldn't want to only listen to her voice and never have the opportunity to hear Sade or Anita. I am sure the same is true for you and your list of favorite singers. Each one of these awesome singers brings a

> *"Your Genius Potential Is The Answer To A Brighter Future."*

different *Genius Potential* to the mic. Remember when I told you my major reason for writing this book was because I heard Jim Rohn say it takes many voices. I learned this lesson during my trip to Ghana. Somehow the organizers for this conference heard me speak and wanted to invite me to speak at their conference. I was overwhelmed as I said earlier, but at the same time felt inadequate. When I met my host, I kept asking them about other speakers, really trying to find out why I was selected. I repeatedly asked "Have you heard of this speaker or that speaker." My host looked me in the eye and said "We have never heard of those speakers, but we have heard of Will Moreland." His response stopped me dead in my tracks. In chapter two I shared with you some reasons people doubt themselves and comparing yourself to others was on that list. I learned to appreciate what I bring to the table.

I was comparing myself to other speakers, instead of realizing I am unique. It is my uniqueness that sets me a part and gives me the opportunity to obtain significance in life and chart my own course in life. Developing your *Genius Potential* puts you in the path of opportunity, "I returned and saw under the sun, that the race is not to the swift, nor the battle to the strong, neither yet bread to the wise, nor yet riches to men of understanding, nor yet favour to men of skill; but time and chance happeneth to them all (Ecclesiastes 9:11).

"Your Genius Potential Sets You A Part."

Developing your *Genius Potential* gives you the chance to finish BIG, finish satisfied and finish fulfilled. When you make the decision to develop your *Genius Potential* there is a promise attached to your development. Look what King Solomon says,

"A gift is as a precious stone in the eyes of him that hath it: whithersoever it turneth, it prospereth." (Proverbs 17:8)

The problem I find with most people is that they usually do not see their *Genius Potential* as special or unique. I know I didn't at first. Because I didn't see my *Genius Potential* as special, I looked upon it as something common. I assumed everyone knew what I knew, and they were just choosing to go against the grain. Here are a few curses that go along with your *Genius Potential.*

1. We commonly think that the knowledge or genius we have is common to everyone else.

2. We assume everyone knows the same thing we do.

3. We phrase ideas as they exist in our own mind, instead of expressing them in a way that appeals to the minds of others.

When I was a college professor I had to learn a few things. First, my passion for learning was not shared by everyone. Secondly, the concepts I taught that came easy to me may be challenging to others and. Lastly, I had to learn how to break down information to receivable parts for others to grasp. This was all a part of me developing my *Genius Potential*. Have you ever gone to the doctor's office and when the doctor began to explain the situation, you had a blank stare on your face. Once the doctor finished, you had to say, doctor break it down or make it plain? Have you ever experienced a cephalgia before? I'm sure you have, you just know it by its common name, headache. Each *Genius Potential* has its own language, so through development you learn how to offer your *Genius Potential* that others may enjoy.

When I sit across from my tax genius and he is a genius, I look with a blank stare for hours. Waiting for him to get to the all important part, how much do I owe or how much am I getting back. But sitting across from him, brings me great joy, because he comes alive when he starts talking about numbers and how I can do this, and how I can do that.

> *"Releasing Your Genius Potential Is Your Gift Back To The World."*

He absolutely loves it. Preparing taxes is actually not his *Genius Potential*; his *Genius Potential* is his ability to work with complex documents and numbers. What he learned to do was place his *Genius Potential* in the right place. We will talk about that in Chapter Eight, where to release your *Genius Potential*.

Your *Genius Potential* is your gift back to the world as I said earlier. And if you are the type of person I believe you are, you want to offer your *Genius Potential* with excellence. You want to serve people from a platform of excellence. Excellence is not perfection; neither is operating from your *Genius Potential*. I'm not talking about being perfect. You may have heard that old saying "Practice makes perfect." That is untrue, practice makes better and that is only if you are practicing the right thing correctly. If you are a beginning golfer and you go out and practice a poor swing, you won't be better, you are just enhancing a bad golf swing.

Learn From The Journey

When we develop our *Genius Potential* we are working to bring out the best capabilities and possibilities. Identifying your *Genius Potential* is not enough. I mentioned Allyson Byrd as one of my *"Everyday Geniuses."* Allyson's *Genius Potential* is helping men and women discover true success through a holistic approach to life.

Allyson is living her *Genius Potential* on a day to day basis. Earlier I said that I believed that all the obstacles, trials and test we face work to help us discover our *Genius Potential*. I believe Allyson was able to locate her *Genius Potential* this way as well. In her own words,

"My father went to prison when I was four-years-old and left my life when I was 12-years old. I had a single mother that dealt with depression,

addiction and financial instability. I was a suicidal teen, dropped out of high school at 15-years-old and weighed over 300 pounds by the age of twenty one. If anyone had a reason NOT to succeed, that would be me."

Allyson is able to use her past to help other hurting people and give them hope to keep living. When we look at the obstacles we face and all the things we have overcome, you can see your *Genius Potential* at work benefiting you. Allyson has been able to help thousands around the world. What if Allyson decided she wasn't going to live from her *Genius Potential*? How many people would that affect? When you help change a life it has a ripple effect.

Let's say Allyson touches 3,000 people in her life time. But those 3,000 people have a spouse. That becomes 6,000 people she is helping. By making them a better couple, she makes them better parents to their two children. Now that number becomes 12,000. The children are able to grow up in an encouraging environment that helps them reach their *Genius Potential*. Those 12,000 eventually get married; now 24,000 are affected by Allyson. Those couples have two children; now 48,000 people are helped because Allyson released her *Genius Potential*.

The more you develop your *Genius Potential* the more effective you become. You greatly enhance the possibility for you to assist more people. That's where the joy and fulfillment really come in, the more people you help the greater joy you feel. Internally we all want to feel like we make a difference, that our life was not wasted. Developing your *Genius Potential* to serve others in an excellent manner is the key. When the Disciples of Jesus asked him "Who is the greatest," his simple reply "The one who serves."

Everyone loves great service, you may not be able to define what it is, but you know great service when you see it. When you experience great service don't you want to reward it? When you see someone going the extra mile, don't you love it? The converse is true as well; you know bad service when you experience it. If you are at a place of service, a hotel, restaurant, Movie Theater or any similar place, don't you get a strong urge to want to report bad service and praise good service?

> *"Genius Potential Is Not About Being Perfect."*

"When You Help One Person, It Has A Ripple Effect."

If I were to give your life a grade, what would it be? Are you a Five-Star Server? Whenever I am hired to speak I'm bringing my

"A-game" I don't have a b-game. Whether I am paid or not, I want the audience to know they got my best.

Ten reasons why you need to develop your **Genius Potential**. These ten reasons can act as motivation and inspiration because when you develop your **Genius Potential**, you will experience them all.

1. To serve others with excellence.

2. You owe it to yourself to be your best.

3. Puts you in the path of opportunity.

4. It will usher you into greatness.

5. Gives you the opportunity to finish big.

6. Someone needs you to be your best.

7. It is the only way to truly function in your purpose.

8. Gives you a true sense of success.

9. You will die fulfilled.

10. Your legacy will be established.

GENIUS INSIGHTS

1. Your *Genius Potential* is your answer to a brighter future.

2. Developing your *Genius Potential* puts you in the path of opportunity.

3. Developing your *Genius Potential* gives you the opportunity to finish BIG.

4. Excellence is not perfection.

5. The more you develop your *Genius Potential*, the more effective you become.

\\

Are You Confident In Your *Genius Potential*?

_____

_____

_____

_____

What Do You Need To Stop Doing?

_____

_____

_____

_____

What Do You Need To Start Doing?

_____

_____

_____

_____

CHAPTER SIX

Developing Your Genius Potential

"Making small investments daily go a long way."

Dr. Dennis Sempebwa was born in a small town called Mukono in Uganda Africa. At a time when the nation was filled with corruption, political turmoil and a horrible financial structure and base. His environment spoke to him on a daily basis, encouraging him to give up, telling him "Dennis, you will never amount to anything. You are doomed to a life of need, impoverishment and disappointment."

I met Dennis Thanksgiving weekend of 2007 at a Leadership Conference in Germany. I was moved by his story and felt very strongly that we needed to connect. This was out of the norm for me, as I know that when you are usually in these types of settings many people approach you wanting to connect and so on. I wrestled in my seat whether or not I should approach Dennis at the break. I finally made up my mind to ask him if he had a card or a way I could contact him at a later time. He handed me his card and I returned to my seat. When the conference was over I headed toward my car and drove the three hours to my home. Once I was home, I placed the card on my desk and left it there for several weeks. I wrestled back and forth again should I contact Dennis. I wasn't sure why I needed to contact him, I didn't see the reason as of yet, just that strong feeling from the conference.

Two months passed by and I hadn't contacted Dennis. It was now January 2008 and I was headed back to Ghana for another Leadership Conference. I made it to Ghana and the first night I was there resting in my hotel room, I turn on the television and who do I see? Dennis! Only it wasn't in the same way I met him two months earlier, this was a singing Dennis. What I didn't know was that before Dennis became an internationally known Leadership Expert, he was the founder of *Limit X,* an award winning gospel music group that had traveled to over 60 countries on 6 continents.

That sealed the deal for me, this wasn't just some coincidence. Here I was all the way in Ghana and I see Dennis on the television. I told myself as soon as I returned home I would contact

Dennis. Didn't know why, but I knew I had to connect with him.

In this chapter I want to talk about the process of developing your *Genius Potential* and the road you must take before you can release your full *Genius Potential*. I haven't mentioned a critical aspect about *Genius Potential* as of yet in this book, so let me do it now. Please do not confuse *Genius Potential* with your purpose in life. Your *Genius Potential* is your gifting, your natural ability. Purpose is your reason for being, why you are here on earth. Being a teacher of leadership principals is my *Genius Potential*, but my purpose in life is to instruct people how to *"Live In Victory Everyday through Leadership, Insight, Vision & Education."* This is why I write books, teach seminars and so forth.

I believe a person can identify their *Genius Potential*, but only God can tell a person their true purpose in life. I'll talk more in Chapter Eight about this.

I bring up Dennis because I am fascinated at the journey he has taken to develop his *Genius Potential*. Remember, everything in life is preparing you for life. Your *Genius Potential* will be tested for authenticity and to reassure you that this is truly you're *Genius Potential*. Dennis's *Genius Potential* is Leadership Development and Relationship Enhancement. After I finally contacted Dennis and we had several conversations, it became apparent why I needed him in my life. Dennis is my mentor and he helps me navigate my complex relationships in all phases of my life. As a leader myself, relationships are the most important thing to becoming a great leader. But relationships are tough at times. How you handle them, perceive them and choose them will greatly affect your life.

Dennis travels the world releasing his *Genius Potential* to help leaders strengthen, protect, understand and enhance their relationships among those they love and lead. Dennis ability to have an enormous influence around the world didn't happen overnight. It has been and continues to be a life long journey of development. Much of it he shares in his book "*Surrounding Yourself with the Right People- How Your Friends and Associations Influence Your Success.*" In the book Dennis explains the importance of identifying who are the Corruptors, Cheerleaders, Conduits and Coaches in your life.

Understanding the journey and course you have been on so far in life will help you understand how it all plays in developing your *Genius Potential*. Growing up I didn't have my father in my life, so the need of male mentors was essential in my life. Today I take mentoring very seriously; I have a natural eye or pull toward individuals that may need to be mentored. Would I have this same pull if I had my father in my life, I don't know, I'm not saying it's not possible, but I know that experience helps me identify with some of the people I serve today.

Have you identified your *Genius Potential*? I can't over emphasize enough how important it is to continue to tell yourself, see it on paper, see it in this book, I have *Genius Potential* on the inside of me.

Write it down.

I really come alive when I:

_____

_____

_____

Development is an ongoing process, with the goal of bringing our *Genius Potential* to a more advanced and effective state. I shared with you before; identifying your *Genius Potential* is not enough for you to be fulfilled in life, just knowing what your *Genius Potential* could cause frustration. Because you will always have that little voice in the back of your mind telling you, you are suppose to be doing something else in life. Think about it like this, when you go to the store and buy ingredients, you don't have a meal; you have potential for a meal. You must put the ingredients through a process. If you were baking a cake, the eggs have to be cracked, the milk has to be poured, the cake mix has to fit into the right bowl and you will need a pan to bake the cake in. The ingredients have to be mixed and beat together to make it smooth and then it all has to come under heat for a period of time.

That's what we are talking about in this chapter. Here is where the rubber meets the road. The thin-line between enjoyment and displeasure. The process allows you to gain mastery, gives you the ability to perform well constantly and not just be a one hit wonder. Your performance will become a routine of predictability. Those that look to you will become confident in your ability to deliver. Anyone that wants to serve from a platform of excellence will have to go through the process of development. Overnight success takes about twenty years! I hope you are ready for the journey. Developing my *Genius Potential* has been a joyous adventure because I understand that everything I experience is helping mold and shape me to become a better genius.

The Bible gives me a promise that all things are working for my good. Whether I understand at the time or even like what's going on, I have the reassurance that it is working for my good.

"The Process Allows You To Gain Mastery."

First things first, even though your *Genius Potential* is natural to you and may come easy to you, when it comes time to share it with others, you may feel a little anxiety. Trust me this is a normal reaction. After given over a thousand presentations on stage I still get the butterflies in my stomach. This is why developing your *Genius Potential* is vitally important; because it will help you gain confidence when it is time for you to release your *Genius Potential*. I am not nervous to be on stage, my nervousness comes from wanting to ensure I am clear and my message is received by those listening to my presentation.

There are five stages that your *Genius Potential* must go through. Take a look at these five stages:

1. **Incompetence Stage**

2. **Competence Stage**

3. **Good Stage**

4. **Expert Stage**

5. **Genius Stage**

Let's explore each stage a little further so you can have the proper expectation of the journey you are getting ready to embark upon. As I sit here writing I am getting excited for those of you that will take the challenge to become Genius!

Stage One-Incompetence

All of us start off at the stage of incompetence, even if your *Genius Potential* is singing, dancing or painting, some of the more noticeable *Genius Potentials*. Once you have identified your *Genius Potential* and are ready to start the development process, the incompetence stage last for about 1-3 years. This is what I call your trial and error period. Learning from other people that have a similar *Genius Potential* as you, is a wise undertaking. Remember, you are not learning from them to become a copy cat or replica of them, you want to examine their process of development.

When I became a professional speaker, I studied all the greats and continue to study the greats. But what I found myself doing was trying to be them, instead of finding my uniqueness. I hadn't learned how to pull from my own life resources and experiences to tell stories. And because I was listening to so many different speakers, my own message became blurred. To become comfortable in my own message it took about three years.

You may be saying at this point my *Genius Potential* is not so much an external genius like singing or public speaking. Your *Genius Potential* may be to make people smile, and I don't mean as a comedian, but the aura you bring to an environment. People may naturally like to be around you. What would your developing process look like? In my experience individuals that possess a *Genius Potential* like helping, organizing or hospitality have to learn how to help and understand that everyone may not readily receive their service.

Let me give you an example. I know a lady that has the *Genius Potential* of organizing. She is an organizing machine; many people mistakenly thought she was a neat freak. But organizing was her natural *Genius Potential*. When I coached with her, she recalled since she was a little girl that she loved to organize, so much so that she started a business as a little girl that was funded by her three older brothers. They paid her to do all their chores around the house. This worked great while she was in the house, but once she was out in the real world, everyone didn't appreciate her organizational skills.

Many of her co-workers resented her because she was so organized. Organization was her passion and it would vex her to see disorder. When she came to talk to me about some of the trouble she was having with her co-workers, I helped her to understand that organizing was her *Genius Potential* and she would have to learn how to release it. Because it came so natural to her, she would come to work early and straighten up other people's desk. Which she assumed would bring them great joy. Absolutely the reversed happen, and they actually reported her to supervisors.

What was going on here? She was using her *Genius Potential*; she was even helping other people. This young lady hadn't learned how to release her *Genius Potential* correctly. This is one of the great essentials you learn going through the process.

As I take you through the stages please be mindful that there are so many different *Genius Potentials* in the world, I am offering a general developmental blueprint. After you identify your *Genius Potential*, research other people that are at the top of their game and find out the specifics of the blueprint for that particular *Genius Potential*. As I said earlier, I study other speakers; if your *Genius Potential* is decorating you want to find examples in that industry. The stages of development are the same, but the "what" you study is going to be different.

Stage Two-Competence

After you have endured the stage of incompetence, growing and building your confidence in your *Genius Potential*, you have now arrived to the competence zone. This is where people are starting to identify you with your *Genius Potential*. You are starting to feel comfortable with the title. This is around year four, give or take a few years. In this stage you are learning your craft; you are developing your *mojo* so to speak.

There is no doubt in your mind that this thing is what makes you come alive. Whatever that thing is, you feel like a winner, your confidence is strong. If you were able to do this thing for the rest of your life it would bring you great joy.

There is a lady I know that I and others affectionately call Mother Peterkin. This lady is a cooking genius, I mean I have seen her in the kitchen and she just comes alive. You can taste the love in her cooking; she is always looking for the opportunity to cook for others. I love to see her reaction to the reaction of people when they taste her food. I don't think I have every tasted a bad meal from Mother Peterkin. Like the basketball court was Michael Jordan's domain, the kitchen is Mother Peterkin's domain.

She has long pass the stage of competence, but to get where she is today, I'm sure there were some early meals that didn't quite make the grade, but as she continued to develop her *Genius Potential*, Mother Peterkin has become an exceptional cook, a genius cook. In stage two you are learning the habits that help you develop and build on your strong areas.

Developing your *Genius Potential* helps you bring out the best capabilities and potential possibilities. Bringing you to a more advanced and effective state in your releasing phase. It helps you grow and expand to reach more people in greater quantities. Your chances of hitting a home run drastically go up when you commit to developing your *Genius Potential*.

Stage Three-Good

Stage three is when your *Genius Potential* has really become second nature to you. Someone could wake you up in the middle of the night and you could perform or render your service. When you get to this stage you welcome the opportunity to serve and share your *Genius Potential.*

Someone's *Genius Potential* may be writing poetry, this person looks for opportunities to express their *Genius Potential* in unique ways. When you live from your *Genius Potential* you readily recognize the chance to serve and share your *Genius Potential*. If you write poetry you may write a poem for a co-worker that is having a tough day. Maybe a colleague is retiring and you write them a poem. It's not always about being on center stage, you simply love what you do and will release your *Genius Potential* whenever possible.

"Your Genius Potential Is Your Domain."

You know your style, you are comfortable with you. This is the place you really start to feel comfortable about your *Genius Potential*. At this stage you can compliment other people and not compete with them. Life at this stage takes on a whole new meaning. When you identify your

Genius Potential, your time is invested in serving and sharing it. Developing it is not a task, its work, but it is not a task. Again let me say your *Genius Potential* is not your purpose in life, but I think it helps you understand your purpose. It can give you direction and rejection.

I don't watch much television, but occasionally I will watch something. A few times I have watched the show American Idol and I cringe to see how many people have not identified their *Genius Potential*. American Idol is a singing competition for singers that have potential to have a professional career, but it is interesting to see how many "shower singers" come to try out for the show. You know what a "shower singer" is right? People that should only sing in the privacy of their own showers at home with the door closed.

Our society is so over run with the media high lighting certain industries, many people believe they can be successful in only those few industries. So they are willing to embarrass themselves on national television, trying to occupy a spot that is not theirs. This is why identifying your *Genius Potential* is so critical. Without doing so you will waste precious years of your life.

To see the reaction of the people when the judges tell them that they are not cut out for this arena, many of them get downright ugly. These individuals haven't identified their *Genius*

Potential. In some cases they have identified their *Genius Potential*, but they are releasing their *Genius Potential* in the wrong place. Getting to the good stage will take you around seven focused and disciplined years to achieve, but it will help you place your *Genius Potential* in the right location.

Stage Four- Expert

To reach the level of expert, it takes about ten years of deliberate practice. Practice focused in the right areas. There have been extensive studies done in this area and almost everyone agrees that it takes ten tears or 10,000 hours of the right practice and proper habits to reach expert.

Let me explain further what I mean by deliberate and focused practice. When I knew my *Genius Potential* was teaching and specifically on the subject of leadership, business and personal development, all my studying and research turned to these subjects. I don't invest time into many other subjects than these; I allow others to mentor me in other vital areas of my life, because they have done the developing in those areas such as relationships, finances and so forth. Over the last ten years or so, I have read over 3900 articles on leadership , business and personal development, 500 books, numerous magazine articles, listened to close to 200 mp3 audio recordings on the subjects and read over 1000 Bios of successful people.

These files are all stored on an external drive, organized for quick reference when I need them. For many of the books I read, I will write out a quick summary of the book to easily reference back to the book when needed. I don't share this with you to impress you, but to impress upon you the type of focus I am talking about. And this is all study outside of what was required to receive my various degrees.

Focusing your energy, time and efforts in the right direction will pay off great dividends in the long run. There are no *"Jack of All Trades"* that reach this level, only focused and disciplined people reach this stage. You may be saying my *Genius Potential* is being a giver or working with plants, do I still need to put in this type of effort and time? The answer is totally up to you. Let's say you wanted to maximize your giving potential, it is still necessary for you to develop and learn the best ways to do so.

I believe each of us become teachers to someone else coming behind us. So it is essential for you to develop. This enables you to share with those that look up to you as a mentor or as a source of inspiration as they travel their genius road target. Commit yourself to developing your *Genius Potential*, you will not regret it.

Stage Five-Genius

The **Genius Stage** is what I say life is all about. Achieving this stage is when you know what you are to be doing and giving back to humanity. Stress levels are down because you no longer are looking to impress people, but improve people by serving and sharing your *Genius Potential* through your purpose. You will find a person at this stage has a calm and peace about them, not easily moved or bothered. They only stress about the sense of urgency they feel to serve and share their *Genius Potential*. Not stressing in a negative sense, they just believe what they have to offer is beneficial to others.

Receiving awards, being recognized for what you do and your achievements are a great feeling. But at this level, your enjoyment comes from a total internal place. Waking up each morning with the opportunity to do what you love is reward enough. Rewards are not your motivation at this point in life; they are nice, but not needed. If your *Genius Potential* is medicine and you placed that *Genius Potential* in the medical field and became a doctor, it is very well possible you may never receive the "Doctor of the Year Award." The numbers work against you in most regards. But being able to help your patients, releasing your *Genius Potential* and operating in your purpose will be reward enough.

At this stage of life, you appreciate the little things, life slows down and you're able to smell the roses on the side of the road. The amazing Dr. George Fraser, Founder and CEO of FraserNet one of the largest and informative African-American networking organizations in America told me in our interview that his *Genius Potential* was connecting people and bringing them together to build a legacy of wealth for their families and communities. He has been recognized around the world for his achievements, one of his latest achievements, being inducted into the Minority Business Hall of Fame.

Dr. George Fraser is a great example of indentifying your *Genius Potential*, developing your *Genius Potential* and releasing it. During our interview Dr. Fraser tells the story of his father sending him and his ten siblings to the state to be orphaned, after his mother became mentally ill. With little hope or expectation of a bright future, growing up in toxic foster homes and little support, how did Dr. Fraser become so successful. Here is what he said during our interview:

"I inherently knew or discovered through mentorship and modeling that relationships are more important than your education and most people don't get it. People are quick to tell you that they graduated from Harvard, Spellman, Morehouse or some other prestigious college. Wanting to be judged by their work or deeds,

failing to realize, at the end of the day, people judge you by how you treat people."

Dr. Fraser was able to take his *Genius Potential*, put it in a system that would give him a great return on investment and allows him to live his best life. The yearly networking conference that FraserNet host each year is one of the best conferences to attend. The conference is equipped with insightful information and opportunities to make meaningful connections each year. The conference also promotes healthy relationship building between the attendees.

Make every endeavor to bring your *Genius Potential* to this stage, your sense of fulfillment will be over whelming, the example you set for others will be inspiring and the legacy you leave will be enduring. I can enjoy more of life at this level. I truly appreciate others contributions to the planet and I'm not jealous or envious of anyone. I am totally ok with who I am. Constantly sharpening my *Genius Potential* to ensure I release the best of me.

There are five keys to effective *Genius Potential* development. Implement them into your development process and watch your results soar. Being committed to continual growth is going to set you apart from others who still don't see the value in putting in this type of development. It amazes me how many people invest so little in their growth, I'm glad you are different; you are reading this book so I know you are a genius waiting to be released. Read these ideas several times to yourself. I would suggest you write them down on a 3x5 card.

Commit to these five ideas:

1. **Correct practice under the eye of an instructor.**

2. **Training in your Genius Potential.**

3. **Mentorship.**

4. **Failing.**

5. **Focus.**

Correct Practice Under the Eye of an Instructor.

When I began to speak publicly I joined an organization to help me develop my technique and become comfortable speaking in public and speaking on short notice. There were certain things that I did and said while speaking that I didn't even realize that I was doing. When I joined this group there were instructors that were able to point out certain flaws and correct them. As great as the World Champion Boxer Muhammad Ali was, he had a trainer. The trainer was able to show Ali how to use his natural ability more effectively. Although this organization helped me greatly, it was equally important that I found my own voice and style.

Training In Your Genius Potential

This is critical right here. Train in the area you want to become better in. I would never waste time playing a video game for hours upon hours if it had nothing to do with developing my *Genius Potential*. You must commit time if you want to become genius and release your *Genius Potential* in a maximized way. Becoming genius is not for uncommitted people. I have learned that we are all equal in time, but are made different by what we do with our time. Not one person gets more time than another. The wealthiest person in the world cannot buy more time. Learn to invest your time wisely.

Mentoring

Having a mentor will save you many nights of anger, frustration and disappointments along your journey. The richness of having someone that has traveled the road you are traveling will add years to your life. Allowing you to navigate the process a lot smoother on your journey. When I joined the military, I selected a mentor. I didn't term this individual as a mentor at the time; I just knew he had what I wanted. I liked how he wore his uniform, how his boots were shined and the rank on his collar. I started asking him a million questions about the Army, and what

I needed to do to get to his level. He laid out a blue print for me to follow. Make sure you find a mentor.

"We Are All Equal In Time, Separated By What We Do With Our Time."

Failing

Failing is simply a part of the process so get use to it. In life you can't stop the rain; you can only be prepared for it. Failing is growing! Failing is improving! How can I say that right? If you have ever lifted weights then you are familiar with the term muscle failure. When you have reached muscle failure, your muscles are ready to grow. I have learned more in my failures over the years; then I have from my successes. Very few people analyze their wins, but we examine everything when we fail. So since failure is a part of the process, then you must train yourself to find the lesson. Learn the lesson and move on.

Focus

There are billions of things calling for your attention each day. Your ability to remain focus on becoming the best you will be your challenge. I love speaking, I hate reading and studying. I would much rather be on the beach eating some pistachio- nut ice cream. But this practice would not help prepare me to be my best. To be honest with you, I hate the process, but I love the results. I don't think many people like to work out. It is the results they like; it's what they see in the mirror that makes them go back. When I come down from giving a presentation and hear someone say that was so plain and simple, really clear, I really can use that information; that makes me continue to work out. Remember to stay Fixed On Continued Unique Service!

When you commit to the "**RIGHT**" development of your *Genius Potential*, your results will soar. The Law of Success will answer you with the result of great success. God promises that your efforts will be rewarded.

"A man's gift maketh room for him, and bringeth him before great men." (Proverbs 18:16)

GENIUS INSIGHTS

1. Purpose is your reason for living.

2. You can identify your *Genius Potential*, but God gives purpose.

3. Anyone who wants to serve from an excellent platform has to go through the process.

4. Focus your time, energy and efforts in the right direction.

5. Development is a life long process.

6. Failing is growth.

7. We are all equal in time, separated by what we do with it.

Can You Think of Someone Who is Passionate?

_____

_____

_____

_____

What Do You Admire About Them?

_____

_____

_____

_____

Can You List What Their Daily Habits Are?

_____

_____

_____

_____

CHAPTER SEVEN

Don't Despise Your Genius Potential

"Who you see when you look in the mirror, determines who walks out the door."

This is one of the most important chapters because this chapter talks about a subject that I see all too often. We are all so unique, fearfully and wonderfully made. Each of us are designed to add our specialness to the sauce of life. When I travel around the world I see people who have given up, lost sight of the bigger picture. People are in search of something external, not realizing that what they are looking for is right on the inside. There are many reasons why a person would live a life filled with un-fulfillment. Life hasn't turned out like they imagined it would turn out. Maybe people have disappointed them or they experienced being laid off. Various reasons occur to make a person choose to give up, but hopefully that's not you.

I love to read the poem *Mother To Son* by Langston Hughes. The words still ring true; there is still reason to keep going on.

Well, son, I'll tell you:
Life for me ain't been no crystal stair.
It's had tacks in it,
And splinters,
And boards torn up,
And places with no carpet on the floor --
Bare.
But all the time
I'se been a-climbin' on,
And reachin' landin's,
And turnin' corners,
And sometimes goin' in the dark
Where there ain't been no light.
So boy, don't you turn back.
Don't you set down on the steps
'Cause you finds it's kinder hard.
Don't you fall now --
For I'se still goin', honey,
I'se still climbin',
And life for me ain't been no crystal stair.

Believe in that small still voice that tells you to take a chance on yourself. I tell myself often that my *Genius Potential* will produce everything I desire in life, if I stay aligned with my purpose, continue to be focused and never give up. In spite of the haters, doubters or naysayers you keep pushing forward.

Dr. Peter J. Daniels asserts in his book *"Miss Philips, You Were Wrong"*, "How many lives have been lost to the timid waters of mediocrity or the dark doorways of crime because of statements made by those who do not know or because people who use their positions of power incorrectly or inadvisably."

Dr. Daniels was told by Miss. Philips his elementary school teacher that he wouldn't amount to anything. That he would most likely end up in jail or be dead. He performed badly in school to the point where he dropped out. His life looked like it was headed down a road of despair, after failing in business several times and was told the world wasn't meant for people like him. Defying all the odds, skeptics and bad wishers, today Dr. Daniels is a world renowned consultant for businesses, organizations and governments frequently being called upon to turn around failing companies.

Dr. Daniels shared with me one evening that a company paid him one million dollars for a one hour consultation. This from an individual that many said would waste away. What was the key essential that turned it around for Dr. Daniels? He became aware of his *Genius Potential* and never gave up on himself.

Your *Genius Potential* is the answer to you transforming your life. I whole heartily believe that when you identify your *Genius Potential* and began to serve others with it, God will direct you into your overall purpose. Just start serving. Be willing to go through the process, never despise your *Genius Potential* or try to compare it to others, you are one of a kind.

I am fully aware that my *Genius Potential* is a gift; I did nothing to deserve it; that was up to my Creator. The creator, designer or manufacture gets to decide a purpose of a thing, it is my part to accept and bring my *Genius Potential* to a place of excellence. Before you or I made a mistake in life, our *Genius Potential* and purpose was already laid out. Your actions may delay you walking in your purpose and releasing your *Genius Potential*, but it belongs to you. Learn to celebrate yourself and your *Genius Potential*.

"Celebrate Yourself And Your Genius Potential."

Norman Vincent Peale one of the most influential clergymen of his time and author of forty-six books writes in his international best-seller *"The Power of Positive Thinking"*:

"Altogether too many people are defeated by the everyday problems of life. They go struggling, perhaps even whining, through their days with a sense of dull resentment at

what they consider the "bad breaks" life has given them. In a sense there may be such a thing as "the breaks" in this life, but there is also a spirit and method by which we can control and even determine those breaks. It is a pity that people should let themselves be defeated by the problems, cares, and difficulties of human existence, and it is also quite unnecessary."

We are so interconnected, I don't know if we are aware of just how connected we are. When I think about how I and my mentor Dennis met it just amazes me. He being born in Uganda, I from Compton and our paths cross in Germany. We started our journeys from different parts of the world, our paths were different in some regards, but here we are today. We both encourage each other through our unique *Genius Potential*.

Someone somewhere needs your *Genius Potential* to be released. Whatever your *Genius Potential* is, don't look down and low on it, don't despise it. The Apostle Paul had the right attitude toward his *Genius Potential*, "For I speak to you Gentiles, inasmuch as I am the Apostle of the Gentiles, I magnify mine office:" (Romans 11:13).

When you despise your *Genius Potential*, there are five negative outcomes. I have identified these five negative outcomes you are doing when you despise your *Genius Potential*.

Here are the results of despising your *"Genius Potential"*:

1. **You doubt God.**

2. **You forfeit your right to fulfillment.**

3. **You rob humanity of your unique gift.**

4. **You rob your posterity of your legacy.**

5. **You doom yourself to a dull life.**

You Doubt God

When you despise your *Genius Potential*, you are actually telling God He didn't give you enough. That he was unfair when issuing out gifts. You are saying that God cheated you. I can't sing a lick, so I will never be an Anita Baker, but she will never be a Will Moreland.

You Forfeit Your Right to Fulfillment

You can only experience true fulfillment doing what you were designed to do in life. When you compare yourself to others or wish you had someone else's *Genius Potential*, you cannot effectively identify, develop and release yours.

You Rob Humanity of Your Unique Gift

There are literally millions of different types of fish. What if the gold fish swam around all day wishing that it was a whale? Or the shark wishing it was a jelly fish, they would be wishing on factors that they cannot change, so they are wasting their time. I love going into a restaurant and seeing a fish tank. It wouldn't work so well if all fish were whales now would it. The world needs YOU! So be YOU!!!

You Rob Your Posterity of Your Legacy

You are to make a deposit for the generations that are coming behind you. I hope my children and great-great grand children can be proud of the legacy I have left them. By developing and releasing my *Genius Potential* I am leaving them the best of me.

You Doom Yourself to a Dull Life

When you live from your *Genius Potential* you come alive. Every day is a new adventure. The stories you can collect, the people you meet. The lives you impact all produce a great life for you. But when you live wishing you were someone else or had another *Genius Potential* you will always live under your potential. Know that you were equipped with the right stuff to be the best you possible. Never think you were short changed in the genius department.

I think it is a great time to remind yourself again:

I really come alive when I,

_____

_____

_____

_____

Doesn't it feel great to proclaim what you are to give to the world? Every farmer knows that if the best seeds are planted you can expect the best harvest. When you give the world the best you, you can expect the best in return. Look forward to great things happening for you; look forward to meeting new and positive people. The Universe is ready to respond to you. Because you are developing your *Genius Potential* expect your horizon to shine.

Live Your Life To Inspire Others

Lisa Nicole Bell is an amazing young woman that is releasing her *Genius Potential* in a massive way. I am always set on fire when I speak with Lisa. From the very first time we spoke on the phone I knew she was going to make an impact on our generation and generations to come. Her passion to move the masses in a positive way through art, socially conscious media and just about all arenas of media is truly awe inspiring.

As CEO of Inspired Life Media Group, Lisa travels the world to empower the masses and encourage everyone to live from their inspiration. In her own words, Lisa describes herself as a

"Social change agent contained in the mind of a visionary, the heart of an artist, and the spirit of an entrepreneur."

Lisa headed to California from Huntsville, Alabama with a few dollars and a huge dream. Committed to living from her *Genius Potential*, Lisa found herself on national television sharing her message within six months of moving to California. When I interviewed Lisa, I asked her to give me one word that sums her up. Without a blink of the eye, "I am a **PRODUCER**. I organize resources and tools to create things that empower people. Whether I'm on air or behind the scenes, my purpose is to ignite positive action." I loved that answer.

Her passion to impact people's lives and love for media is allowing Lisa to build a lasting legacy for anyone to follow that is willing to go through the process.

Every time you think you are ready to give up or you are feeling down. I want you to return to this chapter and remind yourself that you are not disadvantaged in any way, right where you are, you have enough. I leave you with another one of

my favorite poems by Edgar A. Guest, called
Equipment:

Figure it out for yourself, my lad.
You've got all that the greatest of men have
had,

Two arms, two hands, two legs, two eyes,
And a brain to use if you would be wise.
With this equipment they all began,
So start for the top and say, "I Can."
Look them over, the wise and the great,
They take their food from a common plate,
And similar knives and forks they use,
With similar laces they tie their shoes.
The world considers them brave and smart,
But you've got all they had when they made
their start.

You can triumph and come to skill,
You can be great if you only will.
You're well equipped for the fight you choose,
You have arms and legs and a brain to use.
And the man who has risen great deeds to do,
Began his life with no more than you.
You are the handicap you must face,

You are the one who must choose your place,
You must say where you want to go,
How much you will study the truth to know.
God has equipped you for life, but He
Lets you decide what you want to be.

Courage must come from the soul within,
The man must furnish the will to win.
So figure it out for yourself, my lad,

You were born with all that the great have had,
With your equipment they all began.
Get hold of yourself, and say: "I Can."

"Don't Despise Your Genius Potential."

GENIUS INSIGHTS

1. Your *Genius Potential* is the answer to you transforming your life.

2. Someone is waiting on your *Genius Potential.*

3. Developing your *Genius Potential* allows your horizon to expand.

4. The Process

    a. Practice
    b. Training
    c. Mentorship
    d. Failing
    e. Focus

5. Celebrate yourself and your *Genius Potential.*

Can You Think of Someone Who is Living From Their *Genius Potential*?

_____

_____

_____

_____

What Do You Admire About Them?

_____

_____

_____

_____

Who Should You Share This Book With?

_____

_____

_____

_____

CHAPTER EIGHT

Releasing Your Genius Potential

"The World is your canvas, paint the picture."

Up until this point we have covered identifying and developing your *Genius Potential*. Now it's time to bring your *Genius Potential* to the world. It is fundamentally essential for you to understand how you serve and share your *Genius Potential* with others. A failure to understand this critical element will leave you frustrated and exhausted in life. In real-estate they have a saying *"Location, Location, Location"* is all that matters for you to be successful. Similarly the same is true with your *Genius Potential*.

Your natural proclivity is to want to serve and share with **EVERYONE** your *Genius Potential*, but everyone will not have the same feeling. To avoid feeling bad about your *Genius Potential* or even despising your *Genius Potential* like we discussed in Chapter Seven, you need to know four key aspects of successfully releasing your *Genius Potential*. These four aspects are what we will discuss in this chapter.

I mentioned earlier that your *Genius Potential* and your life purpose is not the same, but that your *Genius Potential* could usher you into your life purpose. Since I was a little boy I knew I would be some type of speaker, some thought I would be a lawyer, public servant, preacher or a school teacher. In three out of the four I have done so far, not bad huh. There was evidence that I would be doing something in life that dealt with speaking in a public format. As I revealed I am a teacher by nature, teaching is what makes me come alive.

So teaching comes natural to me, but how to use my gift was the key to effectively using my *Genius Potential*. Once I was fully convinced that being a teacher was my *Genius Potential*, I wanted to know in what way was I suppose to release my *Genius Potential.*

Discovering Your Purpose

My upbringing centered my faith in believing that God created me. This is my foundational belief, so my process for discovering my **PURPOSE** in life was asking God. I prayed to

God and said the following, "Father, I don't want to be an average school teacher, pastor, politician, public servant or whatever I may become, just going through the motions. I want to have a great impact; I want my life to have meaning and matter." It wasn't in a day or two, but eventually God answered my prayer and revealed to me my life's purpose, which was to teach individuals how to *"Live In Victory Everyday."*

In one of the previous chapters I talked about my personal development and how it is centered on leadership and personal development. Knowing my **Genius Potential** and purpose determined my choice on what to study, where to go and who to connect with a whole lot easier. If your **Genius Potential** is like mines and you are a teacher, you need to know what subject you will teach, math, science, music or whatever subject you choose. Goes back to what naturally comes to you and what makes you come alive.

Remember we talked about the Apostle Paul; he too was a teacher and had a passion for what I will call religious obedience. Paul says of himself, "Circumcised the eighth day, of the stock of Israel, of the tribe of Benjamin, an Hebrew of the Hebrews; as touching the law, a Pharisee; concerning zeal, persecuting the church; touching the righteousness which is in the law, blameless" (Philippians 3:5-6). But Paul was mistaken in how he should use this passion and his energy. Paul thought he was on the right road, but because he had never consulted with the Creator, he was lost, destined to live a worthless life. I want to use Paul as an example in how releasing your *Genius Potential* works; his life story provides a great example.

In the book of Acts, Chapter twenty-two Paul recounts the day he was introduced to his purpose in life.

"Men, brethren, and fathers, hear ye my defence which I make now unto you. (And when they heard that he spake in the Hebrew tongue to them, they kept the more silence: and he saith,) I am verily a man which am a Jew, born in Tarsus, a city in Cilicia, yet brought up in this city at the feet of Gamaliel, and taught according to the perfect manner of the law of the fathers, and was zealous toward God, as ye all are this day."
(Acts 22:1-3)

Paul thought he knew what his passion was about; he had attended school, he was taught by one of the best scholars of the day and had sincere desire to please God.

"And I persecuted this way unto the death, binding and delivering into prisons both men and women. As also the high priest doth bear me witness, and all the estate of the elders: from whom also I received letters unto the brethren, and went to Damascus, to bring them

which were there bound unto Jerusalem, for to be punished." (Acts 22:4-5)

He was even encouraged, promoted and equipped to travel down this wrong road. How many of you are living the wrong purpose for your life?

**"And it came to pass, that, as I made my journey, and was come nigh unto Damascus about noon, suddenly there shone from heaven a great light round about me.
And I fell unto the ground, and heard a voice saying unto me, Saul, Saul, why persecutest thou me? And I answered, Who art thou, Lord? And he said unto me, I am Jesus of Nazareth, whom thou persecutest. And they that were with me saw indeed the light, and were afraid; but they heard not the voice of him that spake to me." (Acts 22:6-9)**

Paul says that while he was on a journey to accomplish what he thought was his purpose, he was interrupted. I hope this book interrupts you and causes you to examine if you are on the right course in life. Also notice that the voice was only heard by Paul, not anyone else, because purpose is always private before it is public.

"And I said, What shall I do, LORD? And the Lord said unto me, Arise, and go into Damascus; and there it shall be told thee of all

things which are appointed for thee to do."
(Acts 22:10)

When God spoke to Paul, he made Paul aware that there were some specific things that he was appointed to do. I know for myself and for you, that we have been placed on earth to accomplish some specific and appointed things.

Along with knowing your purpose the next essential to releasing your *Genius Potential* is your market; who are the **PEOPLE** I should be serving my *Genius Potential* to. I know you want to serve everyone, but everyone will not like you or be receptive to what you are sharing and serving and that is ok. There are enough people that do and they are willing to listen to you, buy from you or learn from you, so don't worry about reaching the masses.

"Purpose Is Always Private, Before It Is Public."

Paul learned this the hard way. Once he had his new marching orders, he tried to serve the same individuals he was persecuting and putting into jail. Many times those that are closest to you will not respect what you are trying to serve to them, they may be stuck with an earlier image of you, that they are not willing to surrender. In high school I was involved in gang activity and many knew me as a gangbanger, so when they run into me today, that image is all that they can see. It is difficult for them to imagine that I have developed into my *Genius Potential.*

"And when he had received meat, he was strengthened. Then was Saul certain days with the disciples which were at Damascus. And straightway he preached Christ in the synagogues, that he is the Son of God. But all that heard him were amazed, and said; Is not this he that destroyed them which called on this name in Jerusalem, and came hither for that intent, that he might bring them bound unto the chief priests?" (Acts 9:19-21)

When Paul approached people with his new message, it was hard for them to receive him; all they could picture was his past. Don't allow people's judgment to deter you from releasing your *Genius Potential*, a part of the developing process is finding the people that match your *Genius Potential* so you can share with and serve them. Everyone doesn't like country music or rap music and that's ok, there is an audience for every *Genius Potential*. If a person likes Country Music, they may like Taylor Swift, but not Willie Nelson, but each of these singers has found their audience.

Read these following verses:

"Then Paul and Barnabas waxed bold, and said, It was necessary that the word of God should first have been spoken to you: but seeing ye put it from you, and judge yourselves unworthy of

everlasting life, lo, we turn to the Gentiles."
(Acts 13:46)

"For so hath the Lord commanded us, saying, I have set thee to be a light of the Gentiles, that thou shouldest be for salvation unto the ends of the earth." (Acts 13:47)

"Whereunto I am appointed a preacher, and an apostle, and a teacher of the Gentiles."
(2 Timothy 1:11)

Paul learned through trial and error who his *Genius Potential* was for, at the end of the day, he was convinced that he was a teacher that was suppose to teach to the Gentiles. This information allowed him to know where to travel, with whom he should associate with and how he invested his time.

So the first two essentials to releasing your *Genius Potential* are:

1. **Finding out your PURPOSE.**
2. **Know the PEOPLE you should serve.**

The next essential we want to look at is where do I **PLACE** my *Genius Potential*. Knowing where to share and serve is just as vital as knowing who to serve. You can know your purpose, know the people, but be in the wrong place.

"And when Saul was come to Jerusalem, he assayed to join himself to the disciples: but they were all afraid of him, and believed not that he was a disciple."
(Acts 9:26)

Notice Paul was trying to connect, trying to serve, but the people couldn't receive his **Genius Potential**. If you constantly find yourself trying to prove or convince people of your worth and your value, you are dealing with the wrong people. It will wear you down and sap all your energy.

"And they passing by Mysia came down to Troas. And a vision appeared to Paul in the night; There stood a man of Macedonia, and prayed him, saying, Come over into Macedonia, and help us. And after he had seen the vision, immediately we endeavoured to go into Macedonia, assuredly gathering that the Lord had called us for to preach the gospel unto them."
(Acts 16:8-10)

When Paul arrived to the "**RIGHT**" place, he received insight, direction and acceptance. That's what will happen for you, when you are in the right place, the right ideas flow easy to you, people accept you with open arms. People want what you have. Since I have been an adult I have never attended a concert I didn't want to attend, so it was easy for me to cheer, jump and sing with the performer. I was in the right place and the performer was releasing their *Genius Potential* in the right place.

Concert promoters use this same wisdom when they are thinking about bringing their artist to a particular area; they will sale tickets in advance, to measure the demand for their artist. Could you imagine the rock group Guns and Roses soliciting churches for concerts? Wrong place, but take that same band and place them in the Staples Center and you will have a packed stadium.

The last essential to releasing your *Genius Potential* is knowing how to **PACKAGE** your *Genius Potential*. This concept can take on so many variances; allow me to share a few different examples to bring some light to the subject. First, let's look back at the person who writes poetry, should they package their poems in books, in cards, or spoken word format. It depends on the people you are supposed to reach, how they prefer to receive your *Genius Potential.* Take a person who has the natural ability to plan and organize events. Which events should they focus on, where do they place their *Genius Potential*, who is their customer base? They could package their *Genius Potential* as "**High-End**" wedding planners, or as a corporate event planner. If you are a barber what package do you want to offer? Let's say you offer a $50 haircut. If where you are currently located the people are complaining about prices, you are in the wrong place.

Your package must match your target people and place, which is identified by your purpose. When all four of these essentials line up, you get the maximum return from your *Genius Potential*. So let's review how you most effectively release your *Genius Potential*...

1. Finding your **PURPOSE** for your *Genius Potential.*

2. Know the **PEOPLE** you should target with your *Genius Potential.*

3. Where will you **PLACE** your *Genius Potential?*

4. How will you **PACKAGE** your *Genius Potential?*

Remember, when all four of these elements are working together, your *Genius Potential* will experience maximum return

After living in Germany those fourteen years it was time to relocate back to the United States of America and release my *Genius Potential* in a greater magnitude. Much of my developing took place in Germany, but now it was time for me to get to my ultimate location. For me and my family, it was Arizona.

The Woman Knows Her Stuff

Not knowing anyone in Arizona it was essential for me to make the right connections and begin to build my brand in my new city. When I met a few people and explained to them what I did and what I was planning on doing, everyone kept bringing up one name over and over. They kept saying "You need to connect with Mechelle Tucker." She is the Power Networker in Arizona; she can get you anything you need.

Sure enough, Mechelle has been my go to person since moving to Arizona. I love seeing people release their *Genius Potential* in their different industries. Mechelle is no different; she has found her passion and purpose and she is committed to releasing her *Genius Potential.* She is known as the *"Networkers Networker."* When the top people in the industry need anything, they call Mechelle. She has developed her craft to the *Genius Stage* and continues to grow and expand her business 1st Class Consultant. With a name like that, you know you can't play around.

Investing time with Mechelle is always a pleasure. The ideas and concepts she shares with me to help expand my business has been truly phenomenal. When you begin to operate at the *Genius Stage,* you look to partner with others that have developed to this level as well. You can be assured that everyone is bringing their *"A Game"* to the task at hand.

"Have the RIGHT people on the bus with you."

GENIUS INSIGHTS

1. Don't live someone else's dream.

2. Purpose is always private before public.

3. Those that are close to you may not understand your passion.

4. If you always have to prove yourself to people, you are in front of the wrong people.

5. You have been placed on earth to make an impact.

Can You Think Of Someone Who Is Impacting Your Community?

_____

_____

_____

_____

What Impresses You About Their Contribution To The Community?

_____

_____

_____

_____

Can You List What Contribution You Can Make?

_____

_____

_____

_____

CHAPTER NINE

Living to
Leave a Legacy

"At the end of the day what will be said about you."

Earth is a beautiful place, made even more beautiful when we live life from our *Genius Potential* and live to give our best self. Dr. John C. Maxwell makes the following statement in his book *"How Success People Think"*,

"The spirit of generosity created by unselfish thinking gives people an appreciation for life and an understanding of its higher values. Seeing those in need and giving to meet that need puts a lot of things into perspective. It increases the quality of life of the giver and the receiver. That's why I believe that; there is no

life as empty as the self-centered life. There is no life as centered as the self-empty life."

I can't think of a greater fulfillment in life than to live from your *Genius Potential*, operate from your purpose and give back to mankind. Living to leave a legacy puts these three aspects of life center of your thinking. It has been said that the wealthiest place on the planet is the grave yards. Because located in those graves are ideas, concepts, cures and *Genius Potential* that was never released. When you decide that leaving a legacy is right, that it is beneficial and it is the most valuable thing you can do for yourself, family and society, you can leave earth with the assurance that you lived a life of substance.

I think one of the biggest regrets a person can have is to not identify their *Genius Potential,* not knowing their purpose and allowing the seconds, minutes and days to pass by. Leaving them with bags of could've, should've and would've to lament over. This book is not about being famous or financially wealthy. It's not about living life in the lime light or making the cover of any magazine. It is about you being able to wake up every day, no matter where you work and still enjoy life.

A New Race to Run

I interviewed Andrea Bolder the Olympic Gold Medal Sprinter about her decision to live life from her *Genius Potential*. After her track and field career ended, she wondered what career path she would pursue. Wanting to earn in the same ball park of what she earned when she was a professional sprinter, she naturally assumed she would fall back on her degree in Bio-Chemistry that she earned from UCLA. Andrea became a sales consultant for a Bio-Chemistry company for eight years. Here is what Andrea shared with me during our conversation, "I was miserable, unfulfilled and knew this is not what I wanted to do with my life. It didn't matter whether I had two hours of sleep or eight hours, the passion to wake up in the morning wasn't there. Corporate America wasn't for me." Andrea was doing fairly well, earning a six figure salary, doing what her parents, husband and friends expected of her. The only problem, it didn't make her feel alive.

Andrea has always been an outgoing person and has a huge personality. I can remember seeing her big smile when we ran track in high school back in California. Months went by as she battled the thought of leaving her distinguished field. In Andrea's words, "I decided to stop being sick and tired and not living a life I enjoy. I prayed about the decision, I had others pray with me and I realized I was not happy being uncomfortable with my life." Andrea goes on to say that she tapped into what had always been natural to her, "I always enjoyed coaching people, helping people with their dreams and visions." It took Andrea another two years to garner up the faith to walk away from her comfortable zone of un-fulfillment.

Andrea found her *Genius Potential* and matched it with Network Marketing. She felt this arena matched her life training, building teams, motivating individuals to grow their own businesses and being able to use her outgoing personality. Andrea today is known around the nation as the *"Gold Medal Marketer™"* teaching and helping others to live their dream.

More so than living her dream and releasing her *Genius Potential*, Andrea is leaving her children with a legacy that says live your dreams, not other people's expectations of you. What a great gift to leave your children and grandchildren. That's what I call legacy living.

Aim High

Another interview I conducted was with the CEO and founder of Ascension Aircraft, a multi-million dollar company in Georgia that deals with aircraft leasing and sales. What made this interview so interesting is that the CEO is a twenty-six year old African American young man. Jamail Larkins begin his first flight lessons at the age of twelve, by the time he was fourteen he had flown his first solo flight. Jamail had identified his *Genius Potential*. Jamail from his own account didn't come from an extremely wealthy family, so coming up with the hundreds of dollars for flight time was a challenge.

Here is what Jamail shared during our interview, "Flying is my passion, so I did whatever I could to raise the money. I volunteered at the local flight school, I washed airplanes, cleaned the flight line, whatever I could do." Jamail says it paid off, local pilots became aware of Jamail having a passion to fly and they would offer Jamail an empty seat when one was available.

Throughout this book I have tried to convince you that when you give your energy, time and effort to your *Genius Potential*, the Laws of Success will respond to you in a positive manner. Your *Genius Potential* is your dominion and the Universe is designed to assist you. Ideas come to you freely, doors of influence open for you and people want to help you. Jamail goes on to tell me that when he wanted to increase his flight time, this inspired him to start his first company, Larkins Enterprises which sold flight training manuals and videos to pilots.

The field of aviation is a very complex field for anyone to be involved in, an especially for a young African American male. When I asked Jamail how he handled the pressure of being in a tough field, this is what he said, "I did my homework. When you are dealing with high end merchandise like an aircraft, the clientele are looking for expertise. Even though I was young, I was able to communicate with confidence." This goes back to what we talked about in Chapter Six, the process. You have to become a student, identifying your *Genius Potential* is not enough to be successful.

Tomorrow's Aeronautical Museum in Compton, California is a top rate training facility teaching inner city youth bout aeronautical careers. When I walked in the building, one of the first pictures I saw on the wall was that of Jamail. His photo stood as inspiration for the other young pilots. Jamail had done his first flight at fourteen; the director of the museum showed me a picture of a young man that completed his first flight at the age of eleven. Because Jamail was able to identify, develop and release his *Genius Potential*, others were being inspired. That is legacy living.

I was proud to walk in this airport in Compton, California, my birth place. The place that had been known as the worst city in the United States is now producing children that are doing world class things. Even a city can turn itself around and become Genius!

We are all put on earth to work with, inspire and motivate those around us. You can only do that from your place of passion, what I call your *Genius Potential*. Stories like Andrea and Jamail are all around. They are more common than you think, especially when you know where to look. Have you ever purchased something before and immediately realize how many other people have the same item. Before, you never noticed it, until you possessed it yourself.

You will never be inspired to develop what you hate or don't enjoy. That's why it's vitally important to identify your *Genius Potential*, but more so to give into the idea that your joy and happiness really rely on you doing what you were naturally born to do. How much better would your health be, life become and everyday well being be if you decided to live from your *Genius Potential*? I think extremely better.

GENIUS INSIGHTS

1. Live your dreams.

2. You owe us your best.

3. Your passion will push you and open doors for you.

4. There is a way for you to do what you love to do.

5. Think and grow rich.

6. Never give up.

7. The Laws of Success is designed to assist you.

What Can You Start Doing Today to Develop Your *Genius Potential*?

_____

_____

_____

_____

What New People Can You Reach Out To For Mentorship?

_____

_____

_____

What Are Some Books or Magazines You Can Start Reading Today?

_____

_____

_____

CHAPTER TEN

The Genius Formula

"Success is a science, it will work for anyone."

I told you I would share with you the *"Genius Formula."* Were you able to figure it out? In each chapter and each story, I left clues. When you apply this formula, you are destined to live a *Genius Life.* The formula is quite simple, but disregarded by many. The *"Genius Formula"* is made up of four simple components, when mixed together and aligned correctly they produce the releasing of a person's *Genius Potential.*

I have learned, lived and taught this formula around the world, 30 countries and counting. When anyone is willing to learn and apply the formula, they identify, develop and release their **"Genius Potential."** I hope you will join the countless individuals that are choosing to live the **Genius Life!**

The Genius Formula

Here it is, when you combine your **Natural Ability with Passion, Determination and Consistency** you will release your *Genius Potential.* Just remember, **N + P + D + C=** *Genius Potential.*

Natural Ability

Your natural ability is that thing that comes easy to you. It is hard or difficult for others, but for you, it is a walk in the park. Remember I told you not to over look this crucial hint in identifying your *Genius Potential.*

Passion

When I refer to passion I'm talking about a crazy obsession. This is the only thing you want to do, you are not hopping from one thing to another. Since the moment I committed to helping individuals *"Live In Victory Everyday"* I haven't swayed. I interact with people from all kinds of exciting backgrounds and professions, but I'm never enticed to follow their course in life. If you are going to truly live your **"Genius Life"**, you must be passionate about the **"RIGHT"** thing.

Determination

As you start your **"Genius Journey"** you will have many opportunities to give up and quit. But you can't take those opportunities. Remember the development stages that we talked about:

a. **Incompetence Stage**
b. **Competence Stage**
c. **Good Stage**
d. **Expert Stage**
e. **Genius Stage**

You will become frustrated, angry and want to lose hope. These are all normal side effects of pursuing your *Genius Potential.* As the old adage goes, "No Pain, No Gain."

Surround yourself with other determined and committed people. Encourage each other. Get a strong mental picture of who you are becoming and the impact you are going to have on your family, community and your environment.

Consistency

Now this ingredient here is the one ingredient that many people try to forsake and substitute for other things. **YOU CANNOT** substitute consistency for anything. This is what makes a genius a genius. Their ability to keep doing the little things, the big things, the things nobody else wants to do. Thomas Edison failing over 10,000 times in his attempt to produce a light-bulb, he was consistent to waking up every morning and going back into the lab. The Wright Brothers being consistent to keep trying to produce a model airplane. It was their consistent passion to see it through.

Your ability to be consistent will allow all the other ingredients their proper time to harvest the results it takes to be **GENIUS!!!**

Apply the formula to your life and see the lasting results. You owe it to yourself and to your family to be your best. The world is waiting for you to release your *Genius Potential*. I whole heartily believe each of you can *Live In Victory Everyday and Be Genius!*

CHAPTER ELEVEN

The Next Move

"Die empty; leave it all on the field."

I met Alex Ellis when we shared the stage in Phoenix, Arizona. From first glance you would automatically think Alex was a basketball player with his six foot five frame. But Alex would be quick to tell you he is the last person you want on your basketball team. I heard of Alex when I was living in Germany, Alex had come to Germany to speak to a youth group on the military base near my home. Unfortunately I was unable to attend the event. So when he came to Arizona I was glad I was finally having the opportunity to meet Alex.

Before the event we had a chance to have some small talk and introduce ourselves. Seeing Alex, immediately I knew why he was qualified to author the Self-Help Book of the Year by the African American Literary Awards,

"Restoring the Male Image." Alex is an impeccable dresser, his creases have creases.

Simply Ellis, LLC the company Alex founded is widely known for the custom designs that Alex creates each year. I was very impressed with his presentation; his passion to reach young men, especially those in the inner-city is amazing. That evening after the event, Alex and I had the opportunity to go out to dinner. This dinner was the start of our friendship and iron sharpening iron journey together. That night I must have asked Alex one hundred questions about dressing. He was so insightful and well studied in the arena of fashion.

As I soaked it all up, hearing Alex speak from his *Genius Potential* was great. I know he had an impact on all the young men he spoke to that day. I know he had an impact on me, because Alex told me about a particular type of garment I should never wear. That night I went home and got rid of all the items I owned made of that material. Every time I put on a suit or blazer I must have a pocket square. Alex told me I am naked without a pocket square, if I ever forget, I hear his voice. When you live from your *Genius Potential* you will have an impact on someone's life.

We have talked about identifying your *Genius Potential*, developing *your Genius Potential* and releasing your *Genius Potential*. So what's the next move for you? Let me suggest a few ideas.

The very first thing I would suggest is to ensure you really know what your genuine, true *Genius Potential* is. Take the next seven days and invest just 10 minutes in a quiet place and ask yourself "What do I really enjoy doing?" The next thing I would suggest is that you find a partner to begin your *Genius Journey* with. Have them get a copy of the book for themselves and you both walk the journey together. And lastly I would suggest you make a contract with yourself to stay committed to your *Genius Journey*.

I hope this book does three things for you. Number one, I hope it inspires you to live a *Genius Life*. I hope the stories of each of the *"Everyday Geniuses"* motivate you. I have so many stories of individuals that have made the choice to live from their *Genius Potential.* Those that I have included in this book should be enough to spark the flame under your *Genius Potential.* The final thing I hope this book does is cause you to "**Die Empty.**"

The grave yard is full of individuals that died full of *Genius Potential*, refuse to join them. The world has been robbed of jokes, songs, ideas, books, buildings, cures maybe for diseases and all other things that could advance mankind because they didn't live from their *Genius Potential*.

GENIUS INSIGHTS

1.   **Your ideas matter, act on them.**

2.   **Die empty.**

3.   **Identify, develop & release your *Genius Potential.***

4.   **Change your environment.**

5.   **Refuse to live average.**

My *Genius Potential* Is?

_____

_____

_____

_____

I Will Do The Following To Develop My *Genius Potential*?

_____

_____

_____

_____

I Will Release My *Genius Potential* In The Following Way?

_____

_____

_____

_____

About Will Moreland

A father that was in jail, a single mother of two and living in what was considered the worst city in America doesn't sound like a recipe for success. Throw in a low self-esteem, a speech impediment and a sense of hopelessness and you will have the beginning of my journey.

Growing up in Compton, California at a time where the drug problem, gang violence and murder rate was at an all time, Dr. Will made a critical **CHOICE** in his life. He wasn't going to let his start determine his finish.

Over the last two decades he has studied and implemented the tools, habits and mental perspective it takes for **ANYONE** to achieve success in life. He has read over 500 books on the subjects of leadership, business and personal development, listened to countless audios and video recordings on the subjects.

Because he is passionate about his message and knows it works **FIRST HAND**, he wants to share it with as many people that will listen. Dr. Will is on a mission to help you "**LIVE GENIUS.**" That means to **Live In Victory Everyday while Getting ENgaged In Unique Significance!!!**

Since 2001, when Dr. Will finished his time serving in the United States Army and was released with an Honorable Discharge, he has presented over 1700 presentation on Leadership Development, Personal Development, Business Development, Team Development and Success Development, to name a few.

Dr. Will is one of the most requested speakers under the age of 40 in America, the author of over 20 books. He is constantly recognized for his leadership, community and business contributions.

Recently Dr. Will has been nominated as a Phoenix Business Journal 40 Under 40, a Top Small Business Influencer and as a Top Thought Leader.

He is the founder of Will Moreland International, the number one company for **"Leadership Life Training Material™"** on leadership, business and personal development material.

Dr. Will is a highly regarded business coach and trainer, working with clients ranging from small businesses to celebrity clients seeking his wisdom on branding, team execution and leadership governance.

Dr. Will is a serial entrepreneur having started or helped start over 15 companies.

A family man, that is living to leave a legacy.................

Services Available

Will Moreland International, LLC is a veteran owned leadership development company headquartered in Phoenix, Arizona. Specializing in customized workshops for companies, organizations and associations helping them achieve genius results. The company has a simple philosophy **"Everyone is a leader and when you improve your personal leadership, everything else improves."**

Leadership experts from Will Moreland International, LLC are available for workshops, consulting, as well as keynotes addresses on organizational development, workplace performance, team building, business development and leadership development.

Global Headquarters

Will Moreland International, LLC
4802 E. Ray Road Ste.23-123
Phoenix, Az 85044
1-480-442-3056

"Helping You LIVE GENIUS in Life & Business"

Request Dr. Will to Speak

Dr. Will is one of the most requested speakers on leadership, business and motivation under the age of 40 in America. Event planners rave about his humor, intellect and ability to connect to audiences from a wide range of diverse backgrounds.

Topics Include:

- Coaching
- Customer Loyalty
- Employee Engagement
- Leadership
- Business Development
- Motivation & Inspiration
- Organizational Change
- Diversity Training
- Team Building
- Youth Leadership
- Servant Leadership
- Military Leadership
- Legacy Living & Leadership

To book Dr. Will for your next event, please call:

1-480-442-3056 or Email:
info@willmoreland.com

Or visit www.willmoreland.com

Connect with Dr. Will!!!

@drwillspeaks

Visit Dr. Will
www.willmoreland.com

Top Sellers From Dr. Will Moreland

LET THIS MIND BE IN YOU, is a great tool to help you develop the right mental picture. Our thinking is critical to our success. This book is filled with insights and quotes that help guide Dr. Will as he pursues his Genius Potential. He now shares with you some of the wisdom that inspires him on a daily basis. **ISBN:978-0-9839472-5-7**

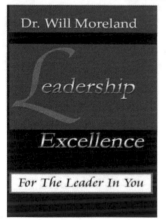

LEADERSHIP EXCELLENCE, helps you grow in the initials areas that make you a great leader. We all are leaders, the question becomes, what type of leader will you become. Add this tool to your personal development box today. **ISBN:978-0-9823944-9-6**

Top Sellers From Dr. Will Moreland

31 DAYS OF LIFE TRANSFORMING CONFESSIONS, will lead you on a thirty-one day mind renewal process. Developing the right mind-set is essential to developing the proper perspective in life.
ISBN:978-0-9823944-1-0

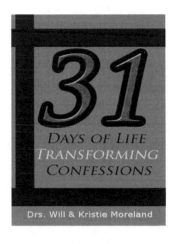

MAKING MARRIAGE MARVELOUS, will help you on the longest endeavor you have entered into in your life. Dr. Will teaches that it takes about 20 years to calibrate a marriage. Get the insight you need to have as successful marriage.
ISBN:978-0-9823944-4-1

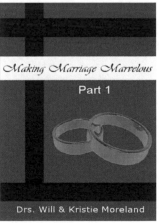

Top Sellers From Dr. Will Moreland

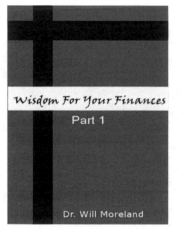

WISDOM FOR YOUR FINANCES, instructs that wealth building is a mindset. Without the proper mindset you will not develop wealth. This book will help you discover the right mindset for wealth. **ISBN: 978-0-9823944-5-8**

E- Book Titles

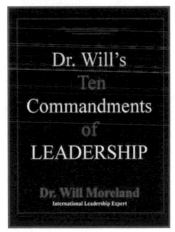

Dr. Will is the author of over 30 books, please visit www.willmoreland.com for full listing.